# GREAT
## INTERVIEWS
★★★★ OF THE ★★★★
## TWENTIETH CENTURY

# GREAT
# INTERVIEWS
★★★★ OF THE ★★★★
# TWENTIETH CENTURY

# JOHN CLARKE

A SUSAN HAYNES BOOK
ALLEN & UNWIN

Designed by P.A.G.E. Pty Ltd, Carlton, 3053

Photos reproduced courtesy 'The Age'.

First published in 1990
Second impression 1990

A Susan Haynes book
Allen & Unwin Pty Ltd
8 Napier Street, North Sydney, NSW 2060, Australia

National Library of Australia
Cataloguing-in-publication

Clarke, John, 1948–
    Great interviews of the twentieth century.
    ISBN 0 04 442285 7.
    1. Australian wit and humor. I. Title.
A828.303

Printed by Australian Print Group, Maryborough, 3465

# CONTENTS

# INTRODUCTION

People sometimes think of our leaders as narrow-minded egotists with limited abilities and no vision. They are criticised for their self-interest and lack of concern for any future beyond Wednesday. Their qualifications are subject to open mockery and their motives constantly called into question.

These hasty judgements, based as they are on mere evidence and fuelled by the tyranny of observable fact, can serve only to put at risk a bold new tomorrow and imperil its proposed privatisation.

Stay where you are and no one will get hurt. Please enjoy the music.

# The State of the Economy

**The Hon. Paul Keating,
Treasurer of Australia**

**Mr Keating, thanks for your time.**

A pleasure. Have some brie.

**Can I ask if you've seen the recent figures?**

The cost of living figures?

**Yes.**

Yes, they're very distressing, aren't they?

**You're not happy with them?**

It's beginning to look as if we've made some very big mistakes. We've taken policy positions on interest rates, deregulation of the currency market and so on and, as I say, it looks as if we were wrong.

**Are you saying it's not working?**

It's a complete cock-up.

**How did the Government misread things so badly?**

It wasn't the Government; it was me. I had a pretty good run for a while there but the wheels have come off. She's cactus.

**What went wrong?**

I'm probably not the person to ask. I haven't known too much about what's been going on since the middle of 1985. Perhaps I should have said so earlier, but when you're the Treasurer you can't go about the place telling people to abandon ship. It's been a hell of a thing to live with.

**If I can say this without appearing insensitive, that's probably not the issue.**

No, you're right. I've got to stop thinking about myself all the time. It must have been bloody terrible for a lot of people out there. How they've coped, I'll never know. It says a great deal about ordinary Australians, you know, this whole business. You feel helpless—all that trust and not a bloody clue about what you're doing.

**If I could take you back now over some of the things the Government has done ...**

Not the Government. Let's be completely clear about this. The policies were mine. It is entirely my fault.

**Can I ask you about the May Economic Statement?**

Shot in the dark.

**Didn't come off?**

Never looked like it, unfortunately. Although, of course, the real problem last year was the Budget itself.

**What aspect of it?**

All of it. It actually goes back to the 1984 Budget. That's where I lost the plot and realised that if I just let the economy run, I might be able to dress the results up as our policy, analyse things retrospectively and stress our commitment to whatever appeared to be happening.

**Is this where the J-curve comes from?**

Yes.

**What exactly was the J-curve?**

I don't recall exactly what it was now. It might have been a reflection of the way reduced domestic demand translated into a control mechanism for lessening indebtedness over time, but don't hold me to that. I'm not sure that's right.

**Didn't it have something to do with the money supply?**

It may have. I don't know.

**Is it possible for the economy to actually change direction, which is what you seem to be suggesting?**

Part of the problem is that the economic advisers and analysts have all been trained by the system which has got us into this position. None of them has any knowledge of how to change it or what to change it to. All we can do is hope to develop a better sort of Elastoplast. The possibility of actual change is nil.

**But isn't it needed?**

It's needed urgently, yes. No doubt about that. I'm just telling you it isn't going to happen.

**What do you think are the main problems at the moment?**

Oh Christ, where to start. Interest rates are appalling, people can't afford to buy houses, we're committed to unemployment, we've trimmed public expenditure so much the place doesn't work, and if the Japanese stop investing in Australia for five minutes, it's all over.

**Why don't you lower interest rates?**

We can't afford to; we're pretending to give tax cuts and that's where we're getting the money from.

**Why did you make a speech recently blaming people who live in houses with Hills Hoists and so on?**

I haven't been well. I seem to recall giving it a bit of a nudge before making those remarks. It's pointless blaming the victims, of course, and I deeply regret any offence I may have given.

**Do you have any concern about the type of society you're creating here?**

Yes, that's very worrying. A lot of cowboys have got the run of the joint at the moment. If you saw some of the mongrels I have to deal with your hair would stand bolt upright.

**How have your colleagues reacted to the news?**

By and large, very well. I've had a lot of support—not from everyone, but that's understandable. There were plenty of people who disagreed with me from day one.

**Who were they?**

Oh, Barry Jones and all those brainy pricks.

**But weren't they right?**

Yes, but I didn't know that then. I thought I had a dream. I didn't know it was just a lot of ego until it was too late.

**What will you do?**

I'll stay in the job, because I've told Bob I would, but I don't know how long I can go on pretending.

**You feel you've let the country down?**

Of course. I've let the country down very badly. Tell the people I am deeply, deeply, deeply sorry.

**I will.**

# A Born Leader of Men

**The Hon. Paul Keating,
Treasurer of Australia**

**Mr Keating, you said the other day you had made some pretty bad mistakes with the economy, that the indicators point to a disaster and that you were trying to do something about it.**

As I said at the time, it's actually far too late for that. We've embarked upon a policy of damage control.

**How's it been going?**

It's going pretty well at the moment. We've spoken to a lot of industrial heads, corporate leaders and so on.

**Have you been speaking to any of the ordinary people?**

Yes. As I say, we've spoken to a lot of industrial heads, corporate leaders and so on. They don't come much more ordinary than that. We're talking very basic motor skills here. They're not very high up the food chain, some of these people.

**Do they understand your position?**

I think so. Some of these people have made very big mistakes themselves, and I think there is a recognition that, as with any other gamble, it could just as easily have come off.

**Could it?**

Well, no, not in this case, but I think that's the way they see it.

**How did the Premiers' Conference on Housing go today?**

It didn't happen.

**No?**

No. We have a snooker tournament in March every year, and this time it was a housing summit.

**Have you got anything to say to the average Australian?**

Yes. I would say to the average Australian bloke ... after all, we've put him through some hoops lately ... I would just say to him, very sincerely, 'Thanks very much, hang in there, and stick with us'.

Incidentally, when I speak of the average Australian bloke, I mean women too. The Australian Labor Party has a very strong commitment to women and policies on women. In fact, the Prime Minister on this very program the other night mentioned the education of girls, which is obviously paramount among them. So I would say to any Australian women watching, when I say 'Australian blokes', obviously I mean them too.

**And what is your platform on women?**

I don't actually have at the present moment a copy of the full policy on women. I'll tell you what, though: ring my secretary, tell her you've been speaking to me, and she'll get you one.

7

# The Idea of a University

**The Hon. John Dawkins,
Minister for Education**

**Mr Dawkins, thanks for your time.**

It's a pleasure.

**You're the Minister for Education, aren't you?**

Yes, I am.

**How long have you been Minister for Education?**

I've been the Minister for about eighteen months or two years.

**How did it happen? Do you remember how it first happened?**

I started off just being a spokesman, having a few views on education—things like the TAFEs and the primary schools, the best way to buy chalk, small things like that.

**What is the best way to buy chalk?**

You get it in sticks, I suppose you would call them, about four inches long.

**How many would you buy at a time?**

If you know where to go, I've seen people buying boxes of twenty and thirty at a time.

**Could you go out of here now, say, and buy some chalk?**

Yes, no trouble.

## And what have you done as Minister for Education?

I've introduced a very full range of reforms right across the entire spectrum of the Australian education system and the curric ... cccricc ...

## The curriculum?

Yes, the curricoleum.

## The curriculum.

The what?

## The curriculum.

Yes, that too.

## What sort of reform?

What I was instructed to do by the Prime Minister and the Treasurer.

## Which was what?

Get rid of the poor. I've introduced a tertiary education tax.

## What is that?

It's a way of getting university students to pay for the costs involved in university education.

## Aren't the universities already paid for?

Yes they are.

## Aren't they funded out of taxation?

Yes, of course they are.

## Haven't we already paid then?

Yes we have.

## So you are asking people to pay twice?

Yes.

**Will they agree to it?**

They won't get into a university if they don't.

**Where are you going to get the money from?**

The plan is to get it out of them when they've finished their economics degrees.

**So, in effect, you're blackmailing them.**

Yes.

**Who pays their fees in the first place?**

They do.

**Where do they get the money from?**

Probably their parents—I don't know.

**Who pays for their accommodation and living expenses and transport and books and so on?**

Probably their parents.

**And who are you getting into the university system?**

At the moment we're getting a lot of people with fairly rich parents.

**Is this a good idea?**

I think so. They're able to go through university with the same people they went to school with and it helps with car-pooling. There's a continuity about it.

**Isn't it Labor Party policy to provide free education?**

Used to be.

**It used to be your policy?**

No, we used to be the Labor Party.

**If we could turn now to research, which is the other major function of the university system ...**

That won't change.

**How will it be done?**

It will be done as it is now.

**Where will it be done?**

It's a vital function and will continue to be done as it is now, in areas designated for research.

**Where?**

Oh, Japan, Taiwan, Sweden. They do a lot of it in Europe, America, Spain, Poland, Brazil and Wales.

**Do you get out much?**

Not any more, no, I can't. It's too difficult. I've got to put the beard on, the wig, change my suit, jack up the police escort. It's just too hard.

**So, what do you do?**

I stay at home a lot, watch a bit of television.

**Do you read?**

Read? No, I don't. Wish I could.

# For Services to Industry

**Mr Alan Bond,
Entrepreneur**

**Mr Bond, how have you been?**

Pretty good, thanks. Fine.

**How are things going?**

Bunch of fluffy ducks.

**You're not worried about the 'Four Corners' story?**

The one about me? Monday night? No, no, no, no.

**Aren't you being investigated by the Tax Department, the Stock Exchange and the Corporate Affairs Department?**

Oh, probably. I don't know. The phones are running pretty hot. There's obviously something going on.

**You don't seem very worried.**

No, I don't, do I?

**Why not?**

Well, I've got the money. Have you had a look at the accounts?

**Yes, I have.**

Have a good look at them. You'll find I've got the money.

**Where is the money?**

Paintings, real estate. A lot of it is in brown paper bags—we hire a fair bit of warehouse space.

**Where does it actually come from?**

As I understand it, it came originally from taxpayers.

**Australian taxpayers?**

Yes, apparently there are thousands of them.

**Have you thanked them?**

No, I wish I could. You don't get that amount of money over such a short period without a sense of where it's come from, and a very abiding and deep sense of gratitude.

**Well why haven't you thanked them?**

I don't know any.

**If you did know any, would you thank them?**

Absolutely. I couldn't possibly be more grateful. It's just a bit difficult to imagine where I'm going to bump into any. None of the people I know pay any tax.

**Don't any of your staff members pay tax?**

I don't know. Possibly they did at one time.

**You mean that, when you take over a company, the members of staff stop paying tax?**

No, I mean that when we've taken over a company, quite frequently the members of staff have stopped being the members of staff.

**Mr Bond, have you ever been to the Cook Islands?**

No, not personally.

**Do you know what they're like?**

No, but I will very soon.

**Why? Are you going up there?**

No. I'm having them brought down here on Tuesday.

**Mr Bond, for the moment, thank you.**

(*relaxing*) As a matter of interest, do you pay tax?

**I do.**

(*leans over and pumps his hand, his eyes misty with gratitude*)
Well, thank you. Thank you very much. I admire the poor. I admire
them enormously. My God, you're an admirable group.

**Thank you.**

No. Thank YOU.

# Matters of State

---

**The Hon. Bob Hawke,
Prime Minister of
Australia**

**Mr Hawke, is it true that interest rates will go to seventeen percent?**

I was unfaithful to my wife, yes.

**Mr Hawke, seventeen percent is appalling. How are people going to cope?**

I'm not going to run away from it. It wasn't just my own wife, either. I was unfaithful to a lot of other people's wives too.

**Were you unfaithful to the electorate?**

No, I was not unfaithful to the electorate.

**What about Mr Punch?**

No, I was not unfaithful to Mr Punch. As a matter of fact, I had a couple of words with Mr Punch before the third runway was announced.

**What were those couple of words?**

I'm not going to tell you what the couple of words were.

**Could you tell us what one of the words was?**

Well, one of them was 'off'.

**And what was the other one?**

No. I'm not going to tell you what the other one was.

**Mr Hawke, why did you spend last week on national television talking about your penis?**

Talking about my penis?

**Yes, your penis.**

I didn't talk about my penis last week on national television. What are you talking about?

**Mr Hawke, with respect. You spoke about your penis on national television on Monday night, Wednesday night, Thursday night, Friday and Saturday nights.**

Well, only indirectly, and I didn't mention my penis on Tuesday night on national television. You go and check the facts.

**Mr Hawke ...**

What's your name?

**Mr Hawke, with respect. Why does the Prime Minister need to go on national television and, on the one hand, talk about his sexual prowess, and then make some pathetic attempt to woo women voters back by apologising for what he did in the past? What's the problem? Is it psychological?**

There is no psychological problem here. Certainly not. None whatsoever.

**What's the problem?**

Well I am simply a very sensitive ... a very, very sensitive ... an extremely sensitive person.

**Why do you get so emotional about Australia?**

I love Australia. I think it's a fantastic country. I think it's far and away the best ... Look, I was having a wee the other night, and I just happened to look down, and I thought, 'What a marvellous, fantastic country this is'. It's just fantastic. It's wonderful. I love it.

**You cry a lot, don't you?**

I don't think I cry a lot, no.

**Mr Hawke, you cried on national television this week. Please.**

Oh, I cry on national television, I don't cry in private, but yes, sure, I cry a bit on national television.

**Why?**

Well, I've seen the trade figures, and I was aware that interest rates were going to seventeen percent. Anybody would cry. It's tragic. How people are going to cope I don't know.

**You get very emotional about women, too, don't you?**

I do get a bit emotional about women.

**Why?**

I empathise with women, my heart goes out to them. I've got a great deal of sympathy for women.

**17**

**Why?**

They've got no penis.

**Mr Hawke, thank you.**

Thank you, cock.

# Australia/US Relations

 **Mr Dan Quayle, Vice-President of the United States of America**

**Mr Vice-President, why are you here?**

I'm here because right at the moment there is a vital conference being held, a big meeting that will determine the future of American security and American trade policy. That's why I'm here.

**Where is that meeting?**

It's in Boston.

**Have you spoken to the Prime Minister about how American agricultural subsidies are hurting Australia's wheat exports?**

Yes, I have.

**What did he say?**

He said that Australia's wheat sales in particular are being pretty badly hurt by the subsidised American protectionist policies.

**And what did you say?**

I told him to go to buggery.

**You told the Australian Prime Minister to go to buggery?**

Yes. What's his name?

**Mr Hawke.**

Little bloke? Silver hair?

**Yes.**

Keeps meeting me at airports?

**That's the one.**

Yes. Told him to go to buggery.

**So Australia is still a valued friend of America's?**

Oh yes. Great and wonderful are the ties that bind our two fabulous nations, no doubt about that.

**Could you be more precise?**

Go to buggery.

**If I could turn to New Zealand for a second, what is your current stand on New Zealand?**

We have a bit of a problem with New Zealand at the moment, I won't deny that.

**What is the problem?**

They're not at the table.

**How do you mean, not at the table? What table?**

They're not at the table. The New Zealanders aren't at the table.

**The table?**

The table. They're not at the table. This is a complex metaphor but bear with me.

New Zealand has left the table. There is a chair there for New Zealand at the table. It has been vacated because they've left the table. But they will come back and, hopefully, resume their chair at the table, and everybody will be at the table.

The table is there and the New Zealanders are not there and, hopefully, those two elements can be put together in the future.

**What would you say to them if they were at the table?**

The New Zealanders?

**Yes.**

We'd tell them to go to buggery.

**What else have you done since you've been here?**

Played tennis.  Played a fair bit of tennis. Played today, actually, at the National … er …

**Tennis Centre?**

That's the place. Played there today.

**Who won?**

I did.

**20**   **By a large margin?**

A very large margin. Comfortable victory.

**How come?**

No one else playing.

**Finally, Mr Quayle, have you got a last word for the Australian people?**

Go to buggery.

**Mr Vice-President, thanks for your time.**

Thank you, and go to buggery.

# An Honour and a Privilege

---

 **The Rt Hon. Margaret Thatcher, British Prime Minister**

**Mrs Thatcher, first of all, congratulations.**

Thank you very much.

**Ten years—it can't all have been easy.**

It hasn't all been easy by any means. We've had difficult moments, as is always the case with a long-running show.

**What do you think have been the high points?**

I don't know whether that's for me to say, but I greatly enjoyed the episodes we shot in Russia.

**With Mikhail Gorbachev?**

Yes. It was great working with him.

**He's good, isn't he?**

I think he's fantastic

**He looks good on screen.**

Yes. I think the key thing is he doesn't do too much. He's very still.

**He's very powerful, isn't he?**

You feel it just walking around with him. What power! But it's restrained, you know—he's not out there using it all the time.

There's such a sense of control.

**Did you enjoy the Falklands episodes?**

Loved them. I just loved them.

**It rated well, didn't it?**

Rated its britches off. It was bigger that Texas.

**Who wrote those episodes?**

The usual writers. Very good writers. We've always had very good writers.

**Didn't you write some of that stuff yourself?**

I wrote a bit. I was really just in at the storyboard stage.

**Didn't you write the bit about the 'Belgrano'?**

How did you know about that? Yes, I did write that bit. That was supposed to be a secret. Someone's done their homework. Full marks!

**That bit was hugely popular, wasn't it?**

I've never seen anything like it. Everybody watched it. You'd go to work and no one talked about anything else.

**Why did it work so well?**

Oh, people love colour and movement. And remember, the country had been through some pretty bleak times. We needed something to bind us all together. It cheered us all up.

**Did you go down there?**

My stuff was mostly done in London.

**Your part went extremely well, didn't it?**

Yes, it did. We extended the show, went to another series on the strength of it ... and here we are.

**Weren't there some people hurt working on that whole Falklands thing?**

Not in the London part of it, no.

**No, down in the actual Falklands part of it?**

Oh, down in the actual Falklands part of it? Yes, I think there were a couple of accidents down there. There were an awful lot of extras involved.

**Weren't some ships sunk?**

I think there was some small incidence of ships sinking, yes.

**You didn't like playing opposite Arthur Scargill, did you?**

It wasn't that I didn't like it—he simply wasn't any good. Couldn't remember his lines. Not very bright.

**Cecil Parkinson's back in the series now, isn't he?**

Yes, he is now. He was written out for a brief period.

**Why?**

Script problems, really. His secretary in the show, the little girl … I forget her name …

**Sarah Keyes.**

Sarah, that's right. She had a baby, and as it was written, he was the father. Well, Cecil didn't think he should have been the father. He was playing this sort of very faithful best-friend character and he didn't think his character would do that. He's back now, of course.

**What's he playing?**

He plays this sort of very faithful best-friend type who is more or less completely untrustworthy.

**Did you think, when you started in the role, that you'd still be playing it ten years later?**

Not for a minute. We thought it'd run for a couple of months, get the family in, a few friends, drink a bit of bubbly, and get off.

**What do you think have been the ingredients?**

Oh, a bit of pantomime, a bit of glamour, good writing, good guests—and some tough subjects. We did one on some unemployed kids not long ago.

**How many kids?**

About four-and-a-half million of them, living up north somewhere.

**This is a hard one, isn't it?**

It's heart-breaking.

**Is there an answer?**

There has to be.

**What is it?**

Run the Falklands again. It worked the first time.

# A Team Player

**The Hon. Andrew Peacock, Re-elected Leader of the Opposition**

**Mr Peacock, nice to have you back again. Who's the Leader of the Liberal Party?**

I am.

**If the Liberal Party wins the next election, who's going to be the next Prime Minister?**

I am.

**If there is a television debate between you and Mr Hawke ... are you with me?**

I am.

**... who is going to benefit from any mistake or miscalculation Mr Hawke might make, even though it might be very slight?**

I am.

**In fact, who's still talking about the last time it happened?**

I am.

**What's the name of the single beat in the conventional rhythm of English poetry?**

Iamb.

**Who's a pretty boy, then?**

I am.

**Are you aware of the revelations made on 'Four Corners' this week concerning the way your supporters got rid of Mr Howard?**

I am.

**When a group from the party comes to you like that, with a plot to knife a man you've sworn loyalty to, can I ask what your first priority is?**

I am.

**Are you in agreement that the next Leader of your Party will be Fred Chaney?**

I am.

**Are you aware that such a move is already on?**

I am.

**Mr Chaney's kept a very low profile during the week. A lot of people don't even know who he is. What's he got going for him? What's his biggest asset?**

I am.

**Mr Peacock, thanks for joining us again. Were those questions all right? They weren't too hard?**

Pretty good. I thought you stuck to the point admirably.

**Not too tough? I could do them again.**

No, no.

**Who's driving you home?**

I am.

# A Noble Profession

**Mr Nobby Clark,
Managing Director of
National Australia Bank**

**Nobby, why did interest rates go up today?**

It's a Friday.

**Nobs, have you heard Mr Keating's reaction?**

I've heard a lot of things.

**But did you hear Mr Keating's criticisms?**

What did he say?

**He said that there was no need for interest rates to go any higher.**

Well, he's entitled to his opinion. That's the beauty of a country like this. You can say anything you like.

**No you can't.**

No, you can't, actually. THAT'S the beauty of a country like this— I'd forgotten.

**What will happen if Mr Keating keeps criticising the bank?**

If he keeps criticising the bank he may have to be shifted to another branch.

**What branch is he at at the moment?**

He's at the Canberra branch at the moment, I think. *(calls to secretary)* Janet, what branch is that character Keating with? ... Yes, Canberra branch. He may have to be moved.

**Nobby, you can shift Mr Keating?**

Not if he shuts up.

**So you're actually in charge of Mr Keating?**

Yes. Mr Keating is a monetarist. Obviously if you've got a monetarist running Treasury, clearly the country's being managed by the banks and the financial institutions.

**Nobs, are you a bit greedy?**

No, we're not greedy.

**A bit?**

Not greedy at all.

**Nobby. Come on.**

No, not at all.

**How much profit did you make this year?**

About six hundred and thirty-five million dollars.

**What?**

Six forty-five maybe, six fifty, fifty-five, sixty, seventy, eighty— somewhere around there.

**Seven hundred million dollars?**

Seven fifty, eight hundred tops.

**Tops?**

Nine hundred.

**For six months?**

No, that's for three months, but we're not expecting it to blow up much beyond that for six.

**Won't it double?**

It could double, but only very slightly.

*(having lost his shirt)* **Does the profit figure include property and buildings?**

No, it doesn't include property and buildings. You'd only include property and buildings in a profit figure once you'd sold them.

**Will you sell them?**

We can't sell them.

**Why not?**

No one's got any money.

*(having lost his jacket)* **But, surely, you're a bank. Why don't you lend them some money?**

They can't afford the interest rates.

*(now naked)* **How are ordinary people coping with interest rates?**

*(bursts into laughter, becomes hysterical and is unable to continue)* Ha ha ha. Oh dear.

**I'll just leave it there. Nobby, thank you.**

Thank you. See you next Friday.

# How You Can Help

**Mr Nobby Clark,
Managing Director of
National Australia Bank**

**Nobby Clark, thanks for joining us.**

Thank you. It's a pleasure to be here.

**Nobby, you understand the economy.**

We certainly do. We run it.

**Will interest rates go up?**

Difficult to say.

**Will they go down?**

No.

**Well, will they stay the same?**

No.

**So they'll go up?**

Very, very difficult to say.

**In simple terms, what's wrong with the economy?**

We have a slight problem in the current account at the moment.

**What exactly is the current account?**

The current account? Well, down one side you've got all the money Australia spends through importing, and on the other side you've got all the money Australia earns through exporting.

**What's the position at the moment?**

The position at the moment is that we're currently importing more than we export.

**By how much?**

By about two thousand million a month.

**Whose fault is that?**

It's your fault.

**How can it be my fault? I don't import anything.**

You're spending too much. The economy's overheated.

**Well how can I not spend? Everything costs a fortune.**

You're importing too much. Are you buying Australian?

**Yes, by and large.**

Your clothes, for instance—are they Australian?

**By and large, yes.**

Do you drive a car?

**No. I've got a Holden.**

Have you got a CD player?

**Yes, I have.**

Have you got a television?

**Yes, of course.**

Have you got a computer?

**Yes.**

Are they Australian?

**No.**

Why not?

**They don't make those things here.**

Well what have you got that's Australian?

**I've got a blue pullover.**

From Australian wool?

**Yes.**

A hundred percent?

**Yes.**

An Australian one-hundred-percent fine wool jumper?

**Yes.**

Where did you get it?

**Italy.**

What else are you importing?

**Nothing. More to the point, what are the banks importing?**

We're not importing any goods at all.

**Do you import profits?**

No, we don't need to import profits.

**Why not?**

We're doing very nicely, thank you.

**Well, do you import losses?**

Import losses? How would we import a loss?

**By running a bond market in Europe and running up debts so you owe money outside Australia.**

Oh, I see—exporting part of our profit and diminishing our tax obligations.

**Yes. Do you do that?**

I have heard of that being done.

**By you, Nobs?**

I believe it was us I heard of doing it, yes, although I'm speaking from memory.

**How much?**

About one thousand million a month.

**Who's going to pay for all this?**

Ask me the first question again.

**Nobs, are interest rates going to go up?**

*(Nobby winks)*

# The 1989 Ashes Series

**Mr David Gower, Captain
of the England Cricket
Team**

*(Mr Gower's face appears at the dressing room door—he does not open the
door very far and seems somewhat reticent about being interviewed)*

**David Gower, thanks for your time. How is the series going
in your view?**

He's not here at the moment.

**Come on, David. How is the series going?**

It's going very well at the moment. Things are looking pretty good.
The lads are all pumped up. There's a good spirit. It should be a
good game down there in Edgbaston. We're looking forward to it.

**Did you expect to be two-down after two tests?**

He's not here at the moment.

**David, come on. Did you expect to be two-down after two
tests?**

Things are going pretty well at the moment. The weather report
looks good and we're hoping for a pretty good tussle down there at
Edgbaston.

**Can I ask you about the English captaincy?**

He's not here just at the moment.

**David, the English captaincy ...**

He'll be back in a moment.

**Do you think you'll win at Edgbaston?**

It should be a good game down there. The lads are very pumped up and really looking forward to it.

**David, do you think you'll win?**

No, probably not. No, I wouldn't think so.

**If you're not going to win, what are your expectations?**

We've got an expectation, we've got an agenda, we've got an aim for Edgbaston and we hope to work towards it and achieve it.

**And what is that aim?**

We'd like to get Stephen Waugh out.

**During the match?**

No, probably not at Edgbaston, but certainly some time before August. We'd like to get him out before he goes home.

**Any other problems?**

Yes, we do have another couple of minor problems.

**What are they?**

Batting.

**Yes.**

And bowling.

**Anything else?**

Fielding.

**What are your batting problems, David?**

Probably the main problems we have at the moment would be Boon, Border, Taylor, Jones, and of course the Big Two.

**Lawson and ...**

Lawson and Hughes.

**What about your bowling attack?**

We do have a couple of bowling problems, yes.

**What are they?**

Alderman, Lawson, Hughes, Rackemann, Healey.

**David, will you retain the captaincy?**

He's not here just at the moment.

**David, come on, I can see you. Don't be silly.**

Actually, we have had a meeting about the captaincy and unfortunately at this stage it does look as if I will retain it.

**Really. Why is that?**

We can't get anyone else to take it on. Unfortunately, the prime candidate is apparently unavailable.

**Who is that?**

Stephen Waugh. He plays for the other side.

**How are your preparations going?**

We are planning to field a team of ten fast bowlers for the Edgbaston test.

**Do you think you'll get who you want?**

We hope so. We've got a hit list of all the ones we want. We're working our way through them and we hope to get as many as possible.

**And who are they?**

Alderman, Rackemann, Hughes, Lawson.

**David, thanks very much.**

He's not here at the moment.

# With Regard to the Numbers

**Mr Wayne Goss, Leader of the Queensland Labor Party in Opposition**

**Mr Goss, what do you actually do for a living?**

I run the … I'm in charge of … I'm the leader of … I run the … er …

**The Labor Party?**

Yes. The Labor Party, up there in … er …

**Queensland?**

Yes, in Queensland. I run the … er …

**Queensland Labor Party?**

The Queensland Labor Party—I run it.

**What would it take for the Labor Party to win in Queensland?**

I think you'll find we'll go pretty close next time. I think we'll go very close indeed at the next election.

**But you had an opportunity this week.**

We went pretty close, too. You go and have a look at the figures. We went very close indeed this week.

**Why didn't you win? It was a lay-down misère.**

I think you'll find we had the ... we had the largest group of whatever those things are ...

**You had the numbers?**

We had the numbers. I think you'll find we had the numbers.

**Why didn't you win?**

Well, not all of the numbers were there, when it actually mattered.

**How many numbers weren't there?**

Two of the numbers, unfortunately, were not there when they were needed in the place where they unfortunately weren't.

**Where were they?**

Well ... one of our numbers was sick.

**What about the other one?**

The other one was very sick indeed.

**Did they remember where they were?**

One of them has gone very close to remembering where he was for some of the time.

**What about the other one?**

Not all the people who can't remember where they were weren't there. Some of the people who don't remember where they were were there.

**The one who wasn't there and doesn't remember where he was, where was he?**

I don't know. He doesn't remember.

**The one who can nearly remember where he was but wasn't there, where was he?**

I don't know.

**Why not?**

Because he was with the other one who doesn't remember where he was.

**Mr Goss, how can you possibly have a Cabinet Minister who doesn't remember anything?**

I didn't say he doesn't remember anything. He does remember certain things. There are lots of things he remembers. He simply doesn't remember where he was.

**Well what does he remember?**

He remembers all sorts of things.

**Such as?**

He remembers the middle bit of 'Danny Boy' and the winner of Race Five at Warwick Farm. He simply doesn't remember where he was at the time.

**Mr Goss, I repeat: why should the public of Queensland believe that you are any more competent to run Queensland than the last lot?**

Because of my qualifications.

**Well, let's discuss your qualifications.**

I'm far and away the best qualified person to be running this State. You look at my qualifications.

**Mr Goss, can we discuss your qualifications?**

Yes.

**Let me ask you directly: what experience do you have?**

I grew up in a circus. I've worked with animals all my life.

**Where?**

Where what?

**Where were the animals?**

I've told you—they don't remember where they were. They've been frank with me. Don't keep coming back to it.

**Mr Goss, thanks for joining us.**

They don't remember.

**Mr Goss, thanks for joining us.**

They don't remember where they were.

**Mr Goss, thanks for joining us.**

I don't remember that. I think you'll find that's not right.

# What's Wrong with Australian Industry?

**The Hon. John Button,
Minister for Industry,
Technology and
Commerce**

**Senator Button, what's wrong with Australian industry?**

How long have you got? I don't want to interrupt your programming schedule. You've got other programming commitments, I realise.

**Hang on a moment, I'll find out ...** *(picks up phone)* **Hello. Listen, do we have to finish in a couple of minutes? ... Yes I know we finish every night at around this time. It's just that I've asked Senator Button what's wrong with Australian industry ...**

**Well, what's the movie? ... Is it any good?**

I've seen it.

**He says he's seen it ... Yes, all right. I'll put him on.**

Can I have a word?

*(hands him the phone)* **It's the producer.**

Hello. Senator Button here. I'm sorry about this. It's just that he's asked me ...

**... what's wrong with Australian industry.**

... what's wrong with Australian industry ... Well, because I'm the Minister for Australian Industry, I suppose. What else is he going to ask me? ... I realise that, but it's not a very good movie ... No it's not. I've seen it. Believe me ... Who's in it? ... Well, can't you just run the last half hour of it or something?

**Tell them to run it tomorrow night.**

Why don't you run it tomorrow night?

**There's nothing on tomorrow night.**

You've got nothing on tomorrow night ... I realise that, but Australia will probably win it. Stephen Waugh will get 280 not out.

**I've seen it.**

He says he's seen it.

**Tell them to put Sam on.**

Can you put Sam on?

*(hands back phone, whispers)* It's Sam.

**Hello, Sam ... It's Bryan Dawe, 'A Current Affair' ... Well, nothing really. It's just that we might run a bit long ... I don't know. Hang on, I'll find out.**

**How long do you reckon we'll be?**

Do you want the short answer or the long one?

**The short one. We've got a bit of a time problem.**

About an hour and a half.

**About an hour and a half, Sam ... John Button ... What's wrong with Australian industry?**

What does he say?

**He says he's seen it.**

# The Environment

**The Hon. Bob Hawke,
Prime Minister of
Australia**

**Mr Hawke. You released a major policy this week on the environment.**

Yes. We did.

**How exactly will that policy work?**

Mainly trees. We're going to plant millions and millions of trees. We're going to plant billions and billions of trees.

**Yes I understand that.**

We've borrowed the future from our children, that's the way we see it. We're going to plant billions of trees. Billions and billions and billions of trees.*(starts reading 'The Truth' Form Guide)*

**Yes. All right. Mr Hawke, other than the trees, what are the major policy elements? ... Mr Hawke!**

*(looks up)* Sorry?

**What are the other major policy elements?**

Well, it's mainly trees, but there are some other ... sure, there are plenty of other ... er ...policy elements. *(goes back to the Form Guide)*

**Mr Hawke, does the environment interest you as an issue? ... Mr Hawke!**

*(looks up, yawning)* Yes?

**Does the environment interest you as an issue?**

*(returns to Form Guide)* Oh, yes, yes, yes, yes. I mentioned the trees didn't I?

**There are some soil conservation measures, too, aren't there?**

Ah, yes. Plenty of those.

**What are they?**

What are what?

**What are the soil conservation measures in the environmental policy? ... Mr Hawke!**

The ... er ... soil conservation measures in the ... er ...

**... environmental policy ...**

... the environmental policy are a very major aspect of the ... er ...

**... soil conservation measures ...**

... of the ... Yes, the soil conservation measures are integral to the entire ... er ...

**... environmental policy ...**

... environmental policy. Sure. *(returns to Form Guide—phone rings, he answers)*

**Mr Hawke, if we produce more minerals, surely that's going to lead to the production of more greenhouse gases? ... *(loud and clear)* Mr Hawke!**

*(into the phone)* Can I ring you back—I'm just doing an interview.

**Isn't the thing that is needed some way of reducing production and cutting back on the greenhouse gases? Mr Hawke!** *(Mr Hawke is now wearing a radio earplug and is riding his horse home)* **... Mr Hawke, didn't your own Environment Minister get rolled in Cabinet over the very ...**

*(The interviewer notices Mr Hawke has gone to sleep and is snoring softly—he throws a glass of water in his face—Mr Hawke wakes up—rubs eyes, shakes head)*

**Mr Hawke, what is the possible point of having an environmental policy that only addresses trees and soil conservation? It doesn't do anything for the greenhouse effect. Isn't this just a cynical attempt to get the rural vote?**

I think it's a very honest attempt to get rural votes—it had better work, too.

**Why?**

It's going to cost a bloody fortune. Have you seen the figures?

**Yes, I have. Mr Hawke, thanks for joining us … By the way, did you pick a winner today?**

Yes, didn't do too badly.

**Which race?**

Trees. Race Four.

# Explaining His Policies

---

**Mr John Elliott, President of the Liberal Party and Entrepreneur**

**Mr Elliott, you've criticised the media this week for getting everything wrong. What do you mean by that?**

Well, you're idiots. You get everything wrong all the time. You never explain anything. You use anything you can to get headlines for yourselves, but you don't worry about the content of what we're saying. Why don't you just explain what we're saying? We're offering a genuine alternative to the Labor Socialist Government in this country, and you don't explain what it is we're saying. What we're saying is explainable. It's not a mystery. Why don't you just explain it to people?

**You want us to explain what you and your party policies are about?**

Of course I do. That's all we want. I don't know why you don't do it.

**All right, Mr Elliott. Now you have an opportunity. We will attempt to explain.**

Good on you.

**Mr Elliott, what would you do if you got into government?**

We'd be a very cost-effective government for a start. The size of the public sector under the Socialist Labor Government is catastrophically large, and consequently very expensive. What we will be doing is making trimmings.

**How will you do this?**

We have a plan, a series of initiatives which we will be announcing once we get into government ...

*(voice-over)* CLUE NUMBER ONE: SECRET CUTS. SECRET CUTS.

... and that would be the appropriate time to announce those deliberations and bring them to public notice.

**Where would you make the savings?**

We'd make the savings pretty much across the board, although, let me say that we would not be making them in such a way as to diminish in any way the usefulness of the public sector in a humanitarian sense to those Australians who have genuine needs.

*(voice-over)* CLUE NUMBER TWO: WELFARE CUTS. SECRET WELFARE CUTS.

I think that's an entirely legitimate function of government and that won't be diminished in any way. We'll be doing it in other areas.

**What sort of concrete policies would you have put in place if you'd got into government?**

For instance, we've got a very good defence policy, much better than the one that's in there at the moment ...

*(voice-over)* THE MISSING OBJECT IS TAX POLICY.

We've got policies in particular on, say, transport, rail policy. We've got policies on *(at this point Mr Elliott emits a belch of Shakespearean proportions which seems to interrupt his flow)* ... Excuse me.

**Mr Elliott, thank you.**

*(to camera)* **No more calls, thank you. We have a winner.**

# Grace Under Pressure

**The Hon. Andrew Peacock, Leader of the Opposition**

**Mr ... er ...**

Peacock.

**Mr Peacock, you've taken a pasting this week. You've run an election campaign when there wasn't an election on, and it would appear on the figures currently available that you lost it. 'The Bulletin' has called you a hollow man—all feathers and no bones. What do you say to all that? The wheels have really come off, haven't they? Would you like an opportunity to tell us what went wrong with the mock election campaign?**

Yes, I'll tell you what happened. On the Monday I was addressing a group of people and there was a woman there with wings who had a very short stick, and she touched me on the shoulder with it, and I was falling down this kind of well, and I got to the bottom and I was swimming, and next to me was a huge, huge, mouse, swimming along, and someone was crying, and then I saw this rabbit ...

**Was it a white rabbit?**

It was a white rabbit, and he had some sort of obsession with the time. He had a ...

**Did he have a little fob watch?**

Yes, he had a fob watch.

**This was in Adelaide?**

Yes, this was in Adelaide, and there was a very small hole in the bottom of the wall and we went through it—I followed this rabbit—and there were lots of playing cards that seemed to be people—I mean they were clearly people and yet they were clearly playing cards—it was quite …

**Was there a Mad Hatter with a big hat?**

There was a bloke with a hat, yes, sitting next to a mouse who had gone to sleep in a teapot. And then on the Tuesday, I was crossing a river, and under the bridge there was this strange shape that came up and began to talk to me.

**Was it a troll?**

It was a troll.

**And what did it say?**

It asked me who I was.

**And what did you say?**

I told it who I was. I said, 'I'm Andrew Peacock, the Member for Kooyong, Leader of the Liberal Party.'

**And what did the troll say?**

The troll said it was going to eat me.

**And what did you say?**

I told it to wait for John Elliott.

**Why?**

Because he's much bigger than I am.

**What happened then?**

Then I walked across and I was on this yellow road that just seemed to go forever.

**Was it a yellow brick road?**

It was a yellow road, yes, made of bricks.

**This was in Brisbane?**

This was in Brisbane, on the Wednesday, and then, suddenly we were aware that we had to go to somewhere in the west.

**To the wicked ...**

To something which was in the west, yes. So we went to Perth. I was in Perth on the Thursday morning, and there was this vicious wind that sucked us all up, and next thing I knew, I was in Canberra.

**And what happened?**

I woke up.

**Do you think it was a dream?**

No, it was real.

**50** **How do you know?**

It was in 'The Bulletin'.

# Concerning the Pilots' Strike

**The Hon. Bob Hawke,
Prime Minister of
Australia**

**Mr Hawke, you've come in for some criticism this week about subsidising the airlines, haven't you?**

Hang on a minute. We're not subsidising the airlines. Who told you that? As a matter of fact, I've seen that in the press all week, that we're subsidising the airlines. That is a misconstruction.

**It is a subsidy to the airlines.**

We are not subsidising the airlines. That's not what we're doing.

**All right, Mr Hawke, but it is a subsidy.**

Of course it's a subsidy, but it's a subsidy to the airline employees, to the people whose jobs have been taken away by the selfish, self-interested group who are apparently bent on holding the country to ransom and running the place into the ground.

**But you are paying it to the airlines, Mr Hawke.**

Only technically.

**Let's not split hairs.**

How on earth am I going to get money to the airline employees without going through the airlines? If you can think of a way of doing that I think I can get you a professorship in logic at some rather attractive university.

**Putting aside my career alternatives, Mr Hawke—you are setting a dangerous precedent. Why are you doing that?**

I'm not setting a precedent. It's not a dangerous precedent.

**It is a dangerous precedent.**

It's not a dangerous precedent. Bear this in mind: one of these airlines is owned by the Government; it is owned and managed by the people who run this country.

**What about Australian Airlines?**

I think that's owned by the taxpayers.

**Mr Hawke, have you spoken to the Government this week?**

Of course I've spoken to him. I rang him this afternoon. How do you think I can be the Prime Minister of a country without being in contact with the Government? Really.

**Are you going to talk to the pilots?**

No. I'm not going to speak to the pilots at all.

**Why not?**

Because they have chosen, for their own selfish reasons, to go outside the accepted guidelines. They have no compunction whatsoever about sending the country broke, and I won't have anything to do with them.

**Mr Hawke, isn't the country going broke anyway?**

Only very slowly.

**Isn't this going to speed things up a bit?**

It will. Precisely. That is the danger. This is a national disaster.

**Under the circumstances, how long do you think it will be before the country goes broke?**

(looking at wristwatch) It's difficult to say. I haven't got a second hand on this thing, but it will be very, very fast indeed. It's a national catastrophe.

**Mr Hawke, how do you explain a poll that we ran on this program, that suggests that seventy-five percent of people believe you are handling this very badly?**

I don't have any trouble believing that seventy-five percent of the people who watch this program think I'm not doing a good job, but let me tell you—we run our own polls. I am in constant touch with feeling in the community on this, as on many other issues. I conducted a poll this afternoon as a matter of fact—this will interest you—one hundred percent approval of the way I'm handling this dispute. One hundred percent.

**Mr Hawke, with respect, who did you talk to?**

I spoke to the Government.

**And what did he say?**

I don't know. I didn't understand a word of it.

# The Old Pro

**Sir Robert Sparkes, President of the Queensland National Party**

**Sir Robert, could I ask you about your relationship with Mr Cooper?**

Mr Russell Cooper?

**Yes.**

Certainly. What particular aspect of it?

**How does it work, exactly?**

You work the mouth with the use of the hand up inside the head, and you move the head around by rotating a little handle.

**Where is the handle?**

It's up in behind the neck. You probably wouldn't have seen it.

**No, I haven't.**

No, you wouldn't know it was there if I hadn't told you.

**So you just open the mouth when you want to say something?**

Actually, we just close it when we don't want to say something. We tend to leave it pretty much open at the moment.

**You seemed to have had a problem with it the other night when it was asked about the Separation of Powers.**

Yes we did. That was my fault entirely.

**What went wrong?**

I tried to do something I probably shouldn't have tried this early in the engagement. It was very silly of me really.

**What was that?**

I tried to answer the question while drinking a glass of water.

**Sir Robert, what is the Separation of Powers exactly?**

The Separation of Powers is an ancient Latin legal dictum.

**Meaning what?**

It's Latin for, 'we'll have a bit of a ring-around in the weekend'.

**What was the matter with the last one, the Ahern doll?**

Oh! Shocking experience. That was terrible. That one was only hired, mind you. It had faulty controls. There was a design fault somewhere in behind the eyes. We ran into all sorts of trouble.

**Like what?**

For instance, you'd say 'business as usual', and it would come out 'loss of entitlements'. It was all very embarrassing.

**The Cooper voice is very much like the Joh voice, isn't it?**

Is it? It shouldn't be.

**People are saying that.**

Really? Well, that's my fault again. I should watch that. I suppose it's just that when you've had an act that has gone so well for so long …

**Stay with it?**

Stay with it, yes. If it works, don't fix it. But I must watch that. Thanks for noticing it.

**Who writes the scripts?**

We have a bit of a ring-around in the weekend and see if anyone has a decent idea.

**What happens if they have a good idea?**

We fix them up, normally by about the Wednesday.

**Sir Robert, would you like to go through the tour details while you are here?**

Sure. We're in Brisbane until October 8th, and then we're going up to Rockhampton. We've got a fortnight in Mackay, and a possible engagement in Tweed Heads about the middle of November, but yet to be confirmed.

**So watch your local paper for details?**

Oh, there won't be any details in the local paper. What do you think I'm doing with the other hand?

**Sir Robert, I hope the tour goes very successfully for you.**

Gottle of gear.

# Retired Hurt

The Rt Hon. Malcolm Fraser, Former Prime Minister of Australia and Unsuccessful Candidate for Secretary-General of the Commonwealth

**Mr Fraser, first of all, commiserations on missing out on the position this week.**

Thank you very much indeed.

**Were you disappointed?**

I don't know that I was disappointed, exactly.

**Well, you weren't appointed.**

No, I wasn't appointed. I suppose I was unappointed.

**Were you disappointed about being unappointed?**

Well, I'd rather have been appointed. I suppose I was disappointed, up to a point.

**Why did you want the job?**

Well, I'm sick of fishing.

**What are your plans now?**

Oh, a bit of fishing.

**What was your interest in the job?**

I was particularly interested in representing the views of the

Black African Frontline States.

**Who got the job?**

Somebody from one of the Black African Frontline States.

**Did that surprise you?**

Big surprise. Big surprise.

**What led you to believe in the first place that you had a realistic shot at this job?**

I was told it was just about in the bag. I had a very big ally in this, of course.

**Who was that?**

Bob Hawke.

**But Bob Hawke is your enemy.**

No. He used to be my enemy. Now he's my friend. He was a very significant ally throughout this entire matter.

**In what way?**

He pushed very hard for me to get this job. He supported me publicly.

**And did you get the job?**

No.

**Do you think Mr Hawke will be disappointed?**

Well, he wasn't appointed.

**He wasn't trying to be appointed.**

No, that's true. I suppose he wasn't quite as disappointed as I was.

**Did you prepare for the job?**

Yes, I prepared for the job in some detail.

**In what way?**

I bought the suit.

**What colour?**

Black.

**Two-piece? Three-piece?**

I bought a coat and a couple of hundred pairs of trousers. There's a fair bit of travel involved.

**Mr Fraser, would you ever do anything like this again?**

No, I don't think so.

**Caught any fish?**

No, not really.

**Have you got any plans for the future?**

No, not really.

**Mr Fraser, are you having a very good time at the moment?**

No, not really.

**Finally, Mr Fraser, would you like to thank Mr Hawke for helping you out the way he did?**

No, not really.

**Mr Fraser, thank you very much.**

*(stands up, has a stretch, looks around—he has no trousers)* Is that it?

**Yes.**

Where did I park my car?

# An Interim Report

**Mr Christopher Skase,**
**Entrepreneur**

**Mr Skase.**

Call me Christopher, please.

**You've let a few deadlines go by this week, haven't you?**

Do you want to call me Christopher?

**Why?**

Because it's my name.

**Why Christopher?**

Because it's my name.

**No. Christopher, why did you let the deadlines go by?**

Oh, sorry. Well, we had to. We've had a bit of a busy week down at the office. It's been a pretty busy time for us, one way and another.

**Mr Skase, you don't have any money left, do you?**

Do you want to call me Christopher?

**Christopher, you don't have any money left, do you?**

Yes. We've got plenty of money, that's not the problem. It's just that we haven't had a lot of time. We've had a bit of a busy week down at the office.

**Mr Skase, can I ...**

Do you want to call me Christopher?

**Christopher, can I ask you what happened to the money that was moved from Qintex into your management company?**

What about it?

**What was it for?**

Payment to directors for out-of-pocket expenses, disbursements, taxi fares, bus fares, sockage, umbrage, haulage—that type of thing.

**How much?**

Difficult to give you a precise figure.

**Give us a rough figure.**

Do you want to call me Christopher?

**Christopher, give us a rough figure please.**

A rough figure?

**Yes.**

About forty million dollars.

**Over what period?**

Do you want to call me Christopher?

**Christopher, over what period?**

The forty million dollars?

**Yes.**

Paid from Qintex into the management company?

**Yes.**

About a fortnight.

**Who paid the money to the management company?**

From Qintex?

**Yes.**

The directors of Qintex.

**But aren't they one and the same people?**

Aren't the people in the management company the same as the directors of the board of Qintex?

**Yes.**

Not in all cases. No.

**Why not?**

Because some of them have resigned.

**Why?**

Because they don't approve of shifting the money out of Qintex into the management company.

**Why aren't these people on the board?**

Because they've resigned. If you resign from a board you are no longer on the board. That's what a resignation is. You go off the board.

**Mr Skase I understand that.**

Well, that's what's happened.

**Mr Skase ...**

Do you want to call me Christopher?

**Christopher, is this sort of stuff going to keep happening?**

That will depend.

**On what?**

On a range of factors.

**Such as?**

Such as whether anyone else resigns from the board.

**Mr Skase, what ...**

Do you want to call me Christopher?

**Christopher, what do you think the shareholders think about all this?**

We are the shareholders.

**No, I'm asking what do you think the public shareholders in Qintex will think about this?**

The public shareholders in Qintex?

**Yes.**

I don't know.

**What do you mean, you don't know?**

Well, you can't look after everyone.

**Mr Skase, thank you for joining us.**

Do you want to call me Christopher?

**Mr Skase, thank you for joining us.**

Do you want to call me Christopher?

**Christopher, thanks for joining us.**

There's a good boy.

# Party Unity

**The Hon. John Howard, Once Treasurer, Former Leader and Ex Deputy-Leader of the Liberal Party, Appointed Shadow Minister for Industry, Technology and Commerce**

**Mr Howard, excited to be back?**

Yes. A very great thrill.

**What have you been doing?**

I've used the time to do some things that I've always wanted to do but hadn't previously had the time for.

**Like what?**

For instance, I was lucky enough to get a drive in the Spanish Grand Prix.

**Where did you finish?**

I finished seventh.

**Who did you beat?**

I beat the bloke who came eighth, from memory.

**Mr Howard, could we turn to unity in the party—you and Andrew Peacock—how's that unity going?**

Unity's going very well. There's a very strong sense of unity in the party now. The party's pretty well unified. There's a lot of unity about—not much else about in the party at the moment. If I were to search for a word to describe the character of the party at the moment …

**A sense of unification?**

… 'unity' is the word I would go for. Yes.

**But you don't like Mr Peacock.**

No. It's not easy, but it seems to be working. It's in the papers.

**But he doesn't like you.**

No. Andrew's not much of a bloke, frankly, but it seems to be working.

**Mr Howard, don't you think people can see this bitterness?**

I think people see that as a healthy spirit of competition in the party.

**Competition? What are you talking about? You get the job, and he wants it. Then he gets the job and you try to take it off him. Where's the unity?**

Perfectly natural sense of competition within the party.

**Fifty percent of the party don't want you, and the other fifty percent don't want him. Where's the unity?**

Equality. The hallmark of the Liberal Party. It's a totally unified party.

**Mr Howard, please. You're stretching it a bit. Where is your support coming from?**

I've got a lot of support.

**Where?**

I have a great deal of personal support from within the party.

**What party?**

The Labor Party, by and large.

**Mr Howard, what's your next job?**

Probably Andrew's.

**You want Andrew Peacock's job?**

Of course I do.

**Have you talked to him about this?**

Why would I tell Andrew? The plan's not going to work, is it, if I tell Andrew what I want?

**But you just told me.**

And don't you tell Andrew.

**Mr Howard, you've just told millions of viewers that you want Andrew Peacock's job.**

Yes, but I don't want the public to know.

**They are the public.**

Don't for goodness sake tell Andrew.

**But they are the public.**

Andrew's not watching television.

**How do you know that?**

Because he's giving a speech tonight at the Cooma R.S.L.

**About what?**

About party unity. For goodness sake, how is it going to work if you tell him? I don't want the public to know. I don't want Andrew Peacock to know. He didn't tell me; why should I tell him?

**Mr Howard, thanks for joining us.**

Have some loyalty. You get me on here and then you go and tell everybody …

**I didn't tell him anything. You told me.**

You're going to tell him this. I've only told one person. If he finds out, I'm going to know who told him.

**Who?**

I'm going to know you told him. And you know what's going to happen then?

**Mr Howard, thanks for joining us.**

I'm not going to come here again. Ever.

**Mr Howard, the satellite's running out.**

There isn't a satellite. I'm sitting next to you. Wake up to yourself. You tell him and I'll string you up, son.

# The Tradition Continues

**The Hon. Russell Cooper,
a Premier of Queensland**

**Mr Cooper, you've taken a stand against homosexuality and pornographic rock music.**

Yes we have. We're going to clean the place up a bit.

**What exactly is a pornographic record?**

A pornographic record is one that allows pictures of a pornographic character to be transmitted by the use of a radio signal.

**How is it done?**

I don't know how they do it, but we're going to stop it. It won't happen after the election—I'll tell you that for nothing.

**But how can a visual image be broadcast in the form of music?**

I don't know, but I've heard these songs. They are frequently lewd—disgusting—and they transmit images concerning acts that are frequently unnatural. We're going to stop it.

**How are they played?**

The pornographic rock music?

**Yes.**

On a pornograph. You wind it up, and it's connected up to people's radio sets, and the sound goes through the wires.

**Mr Cooper, what sort of music do you like?**

I like a lot of music. I'm a very big music fan.

**Do you like classical?**

Yes, I like his stuff. I like Bea ... Bea ... Beat ...

**Beethoven?**

Yes, Beathoving—I think he's great.

**Which one of his?**

What do you mean, which one?

**The Ninth?**

No, his fifth album was the big one, I think. I like ... ah ... wonderful piece of music ... *(plays imaginary piano)* Chop ... Chop ... Choppin ...

**Chopin.**

You play it at one of those big things you sit down at ...

**Piano?**

Piano, yes. And Shakespeare.

**What do you like about his work?**

Boy, can he play a trumpet! I like the lot. There's James Last's music. I've got a fantastic collection of James Last records.

**Do you dance?**

I do, but one more and I really must go.

# A Proud Moment

**The Hon. Bob Hawke,
Prime Minister of
Australia**

**Mr Hawke, this is a historic time, isn't it? The Berlin Wall is down, people are free to come and go across the borders for the first time in forty years.**

Yes, it's a very exciting time.

**The news looks like a mardi gras. Why are so many people leaving Australia?**

They're only going for short periods, to have a look. Most of them will be back.

**They don't look as though they're coming back. Isn't it time we admitted that capitalism doesn't work? It's out of date, isn't it?**

The system works fine.

**Don't people want freedom? Isn't that the point of what's happening? They don't want an authoritarian system.**

They haven't got one.

**Who runs the army?**

The Government.

**Who runs the police?**

The Government.

**Who runs the courts?**

The judges.

**Who runs the judges?**

Nobody runs the judges—there's a fundamental concept of justice at work here.

**Who got rid of Justice Staples?**

The Government, but we didn't get rid of the others.

**Who runs the Government?**

It's a democracy. The people control the Government. They vote.

**When do they vote next?**

I don't know.

**Why not?**

I haven't decided.

**If they don't vote for your candidate, who do they vote for?**

The other candidate.

**From the other capitalist party?**

Yes. There's a choice.

**Why can't people afford houses?**

Interest rates.

**Who set that policy?**

The Government.

**Who makes the money?**

The banks.

**Who runs the media?**

Independent media groups in free competition with one another.

**Who finances them?**

The banks.

**What's the problem with the national economy?**

We owe too much money overseas.

**What do you mean, 'we'? Who borrowed it?**

Three or four bold entrepreneurs.

**Why don't they pay it back?**

They haven't got it any more. They're broke.

**Who do they owe it to overseas?**

The banks.

**Will you be leaving, yourself?**

Yes, next Tuesday.

**Where are you going?**

East Germany, Czechoslovakia, Hungary.

**Who with?**

The banks.

# Concerning Unusual Mathematical Calculations Contained in the Opposition Health Policy Announced by Shadow Spokesman Peter Shack

**The Hon. Andrew Peacock, Leader of the Federal Opposition**

**Mr Peacock, what's the problem with Mr Shack? Is it a medical one?**

We don't quite know whether it's a medical problem at the moment or simply mechanical.

**What exactly is the trouble?**

He's losing a lot of air from somewhere. We've sought medical advice. We've used the bicycle kit. We've done a lot of checks, but we just don't know which hole the air is coming from at the moment. We may have to put him under water.

**Andrew, things aren't going all that well for you lately, are they? The only announcement you've made recently is a health program which didn't add up.**

Hang on a flash—it did add up. Peter Shack knows what he's doing.

**What is Mr Shack doing?**

He's adding up the health policy with any luck.

**How far out was he when he announced it?**

Somewhere between nought and 2.6 billion dollars.

**Where?**

Where between the nought and the 2.6 billion?

**Yes.**

2.6 billion.

**Out?**

Out, yes—but only very slightly.

**Could you explain your health policy to us?**

Yes. We have a three-point plan for health.

**Which is different from the one you just announced.**

Very different. This is a three-point plan.

**What's in it?**

What's in the three-point plan?

**Yes.**

Three points.

**Yes, but what are the points?**

Oh, I see. Obviously we require good quality health services for the entire Australian population at reasonable cost. And secondly, we require that the hospital system keep pace with the needs of the population.

**Well that's two.**

Yes.

**But it's a three-point plan.**

Yes, it is.

**But you've only told me two.**

Two what?

**Two points. You've missed a point.**

How many points did I say were in the plan?

**Three, and you've only given me two.**

Ah! We've got a point missing! I'll talk to Mr Shack when I see him.

**Did you have a good Christmas?**

I'll be having a fairly quiet, family Christmas this year.

**When will you be doing that?**

At Christmas—February 12th.

**Who told you February 12th was Christmas?**

Peter Shack.

# Support from Canberra

**The Hon. Peter Dowding,
Premier of Western
Australia**

**Mr Dowding, you're at the centre of a leadership crisis. What are they saying is wrong with your leadership?**

I think there's a bit of a feeling that I haven't done enough to get Western Australia out of its corporate debt spiral.

**In Perth?**

In Perth.

**Where were you when you first heard about this?**

In Switzerland.

**Why Switzerland?**

I was just there for a couple of days, doing the banking.

**Do you think you'll get rolled?**

I hope not. I've got a great deal of support.

**Why hasn't the Prime Minister supported you?**

He has.

**Mr Dowding, please. Come on.**

I have got the support of the Prime Minister. Where would a Labor

Premier be if he didn't have the total endorsement and total support of the Labor Federal Prime Minister?

**Switzerland.**

But I'm not in Switzerland at the moment.

**While you were in Switzerland, Mr Hawke was supporting Carmen Lawrence.**

He was publicly, but privately I had a couple of chats with him.

**What did he say?**

I rang him up a couple of times.

**What did he say privately?**

The first time he told me that the number I had dialled was not connected and that I should check with Directory before dialling again.

**Did you call him back?**

Yes I did. We're like that, Bob and myself. We've got a very good understanding.

**And what did he say?**

He said that the Telecom service I had called was temporarily busy, that my call had been placed in a queue and would be answered as soon as an operator became available.

**Did you ring him from Switzerland?**

Yes, I rang him from Switzerland.

**What did he say on that occasion?**

He was very helpful. We're like that, Bob and myself.

**But what did he say?**

He said that the country I had dialled was temporarily busy, and that I should leave it and try again in a few minutes.

**Have you spoken to him today?**

Yes. We're like that, Bob and myself. We've got a very good understanding. He's been very helpful. I spoke to him just now, five minutes ago.

**What did he say then?**

He played me a couple of tunes by Andre Kostelanetz and asked me to have my credit card ready when the operator came on.

**Did the operator come on?**

No. Senator Button reckons that's going to happen around July.

**Finally, Mr Dowding, whatever happened to the former Premier of Western Australia, Mr Burke?**

He's in Dublin.

**Why in Dublin?**

Because he's been to Switzerland.

*(collecting his notes)* **Have you spoken to Alan Bond recently?**
Alan who?

**Alan Bond. Alan Bond.**

Never heard of him.

**Alan Bond.**

Never heard of him. *(mouths)* Shut-up. Will you shut-up, you moron?

# Election 1990

**The Hon. John Button,
Minister for Industry,
Technology and
Commerce**

**Senator Button, what happened to the numbers on the industrial policy on Wednesday?**

Oh, bit of a bad day, Wednesday. I forgot my tablets.

**What tablets?**

I've got these tablets I'm supposed to take and I left them on the bedside table.

**What are they for?**

To keep me awake.

**Keep you awake?**

Yes, and I left them at home.

**Does Mr Hawke take these stay-awake tablets?**

Yes, of course he does. We all do. But he'd had a couple before we went in. I'd left mine at home, sitting on the bedside table.

**Is this just during the election?**

Yes, mainly. It's just to keep awake during the campaign. It's been a bit of a dull time for us, really.

**What do you mean?**

There are no issues. There's no difference between the parties. What can you do?

**Did you see the debate the other night?**

Saw the beginning of the debate, went for the tablets, but I must have rolled the bottle over and apparently I dropped off. I missed the debate altogether.

**Were Mr Peacock and Mr Hawke on stay-awake tablets?**

Bob was. We gave him a bottle-and-a-half before he went on, apparently, but even so, he dropped off in the middle.

**How did Mr Peacock stay awake?**

He didn't, but you can't always tell with Andrew. Apparently they slipped a bit of horse stimulant into his Milo beforehand.

**What was the result?**

A bit of light swelling in the off foreleg, but he didn't say anything interesting.

**So, both parties are just going through the motions?**

What can you do?

**But what about the Aboriginal Health Fund? The Liberal Party has taken ten million dollars out of the Aboriginal community welfare budget. What are the Aborigines supposed to do?**

Ten million dollars?

**Yes.**

Off Aboriginal welfare?

**Yes.**

That's the Liberal Party policy?

**Yes.**

That's dreadful.

**Well, why haven't you done something about it?**

Well what have YOU done about it?

**Me?**

Yes, you. I haven't seen anything about that in the newspapers.

**What can I do about it?**

Have you asked them about it?

**No. I'm a journalist.**

Get us my tablets, son. I think I'm going.

**Can I borrow a couple of yours?**

I thought you had some.

**I've used all mine up. Are they an imported brand?**

Yes. We don't make these here.

**What do we make here?**

You know those little things that fit over the valve on a bike?

**Yes.**

The little bag that they come in?

**Yes.**

Made in Australia.

**They don't sound all that green.**

No, it's a sort of a clear colour.

**No, I mean they don't sound bio-degradable.**

Yes, they are. They're bloody near indestructible.

# In Good Hands

**Mr John Elliott, President of the Liberal Party and Entrepreneur, Chairman of Elders**

**Mr Elliott, you're reconstructing your company.**

Yes. We're refinancing and trying to get a more equitable distribution of debt within the group.

**What exactly does that mean?**

It means we need about 1000 million dollars.

**When do you need it?**

It's not urgent.

**When?**

Some time tomorrow. Probably the afternoon.

**What time?**

About 10 o'clock.

**In the morning?**

In the very early part of the afternoon, yes.

**How are you going to get it?**

We're going to sell off a lot of assets.

**Will you be selling off the Liberal Party?**

No. It's an asset sale.

**What's caused this need for restructuring?**

The takeover of Elders by a company called Harlin, which is owned by the Elders directors.

**Will this takeover benefit Elders shareholders or the private company owned by you and the other directors?**

Both, we hope.

**Both what?**

Both myself and the other directors.

**Mr Elliott, who do you think will win the election?**

Harlin won the election.

**No, I mean the general election. Andrew Peacock hasn't polled all that well.**

He polled very well this week.

**But he didn't win.**

He didn't win, no, but for someone so badly beaten he polled very well indeed.

**Where did he get?**

He got fifth.

**Who beat him?**

Four other people.

**Who?**

Bob Hawke, obviously.

**And who else?**

Some back-bencher from the Torres Strait Islands.

**And who else?**

A dog from 'Neighbours' ...

**Yes.**

... and a little thing you use for finding the stud in a wall.

**Don't you have anyone in the community with credibility who is well liked by the people?**

Well, obviously, there are people with vision and popularity and sound policies.

**Who?**

Mikhail Gorbachev, for instance.

**He's not in the Liberal Party.**

We can get him into the Party. I'm looking for a seconder.

**But he's a communist.**

A lot of Liberal Party policy is basically communist.

**Who else are you looking at?**

Nelson Mandler.

**Nelson Mandela?**

Yes, him as well.

**He'd be good.**

Either of them would be excellent. There's a bit of an availability problem.

**The Everly Brothers?**

Touring.

**Roy Orbison?**

He's dead, isn't he?

**Yes, but does that count him out?**

I don't suppose it should. That's a very interesting suggestion. Do you have a number for him?

**'Pretty Woman', 'Only the Lonely'.**

He'd be good. He'd be VERY good.

**Does this mean curtains for Andrew?**

No. If we can't find a dead person with the right qualifications by about Wednesday, we'll probably wheel Andrew out again.

*(conversationally)* **How's your job at the Labor Party going?**

Well, I'm only part-time. Andrew would be the boy to speak to.

# The Reality Is

**The Hon. Andrew Peacock, Leader of the Federal Opposition**

**Mr Peacock, thanks for being here.**

Thank you. It's a great pleasure. Thanks for coming.

**I'm interviewing you.**

Of course you are. Go ahead.

**You've been talking about what the reality is.**

Yes, the reality is. It's very important. The reality is. I've been saying that for six weeks.

**What is it?**

The reality.

**Yes, but what is it?**

What's the reality?

**Yes.**

It is.

**I thought this was part of a longer statement: 'The reality is such and such'.**

No. The reality isn't such and such. It is.

**But Mr Hawke hasn't mentioned reality in the campaign.**

Exactly.

**Mr Peacock, he could hardly say that the reality isn't, could he?**

I don't know what he's going to say. He hasn't said a word about it. He hasn't said it is. He hasn't responded to any of our other policies, either.

**Such as?**

We are.

**We are what?**

We are. Not 'We are what.' Watch my lips, son. 'We are.'

**That's a policy?**

You bet.

**On what?**

On a range of matters.

**Mr Peacock, can I put this to you …**

There's another one.

**Sorry?**

Defence policy.

**That's a defence policy?**

Of course it is. A very good one.

**Do you have any other policies like that?**

Plenty of them. Let me tell you this.

**That's a policy?**

Education policy.

**With respect, Mr Peacock, these are all phrases. There's no**

**content here.**

Come on. You're playing semantics.

**These are just useless phrases.**

Obviously you've got to look at them in the context of the overall Liberal Party Platform.

**What is the Liberal Party Platform?**

The Liberal Party Platform? Haven't you be listening for six weeks?

**I have.**

The Liberal Party Platform.

**But what is it?**

The.

**The?**

The.

**What's 'the'?**

The?

**What is it?**

What do you mean, what's 'the'? It's the entire Liberal Party Platform. All these other things come from it.

**Mr Peacock, thanks for joining us.**

There's another one.

**What?**

Ethnic affairs policy.

**Thanks for joining us.**

It's a pleasure.

**Is that a policy?**

You bet.

**What is that a policy on?**

I'm not going to tell you. We're not announcing that until Tuesday.

**Where?**

There's another one.

**Thanks a lot.**

That's another one.

**I'm going to have to go.**

There's another one, although we're not bringing that in until the second year.

# Election Eve

**The Hon. Bob Hawke,
Prime Minister of
Australia**

**Mr Hawke, what do you think will happen tomorrow?**

I don't know what will happen tomorrow. I don't think anybody knows. It'll be very close. Expert opinion is united in this view. We think it will be very close. We're looking for a very close tussle indeed.

**If you win the toss, will you bat?**

I don't know whether we'll bat. It will depend on the weather and the conditions, but we'll give it a very good look.

**It will be a good toss to win.**

Yes. It would be a good toss to win.

**You batted first, last time.**

I think we did bat first last time from memory.

**You batted from memory?**

Yes, we did. Weren't you there?

**What did you get?**

We got 4000 for 3 declared.

**Who got them?**

Paul got most of them. We were 28 for 6 when he went in.

**What did they get?**

What do you mean 'they'?

**The other team.**

There was no other team involved.

**Andrew Peacock's team.**

Oh. No, they couldn't get eleven people. Only three turned up. Two of them had tennis racquets.

**And the other one?**

The other one tried to run the heavy roller over Andrew all afternoon.

**How do you rate them this time?**

Difficult to say. I don't know who is in the side.

**Well Andrew Peacock, of course—he's the captain.**

Yes, I know he's the captain, but is he still in the side?

**I don't know. I haven't seen the afternoon papers.**

No, I haven't seen the papers either. No idea.

**John Elliott?**

He pulled a muscle, I think.

**Don't people in your team pull muscles?**

No, not really. You're never on your own in our side.

**Didn't John Button pull a muscle recently?**

No. Terry McCrann pulled a muscle. John Button's back went.

**Right. Will there be anything tomorrow for the kids?**

For the kids? What do you mean? Like what?

**Circuses, donkey-rides, that sort of thing.**

There'll be circuses and donkey-rides there, obviously, but no, I don't think there'll be anything there for the kids.

# A Few Slight Problems

**The Hon. John Cain,
Premier of Victoria**

**Mr Cain, what advice do you have for anyone with loved ones or friends in the Victorian State Government?**

The casualty lists are being published every day in the newspapers. All I can suggest is that people comb those lists very thoroughly and search for the names of any loved ones.

**Is there a phone number people can ring?**

No. Things are happening so fast out there, it's very difficult for our people on the ground to get a reliable picture.

**Where are your people?**

They're on the ground.

**Is there any way of finding out the condition of those not listed? Is there a hospital people can ring?**

It's a waste of time ringing a Victorian hospital.

**Why?**

Has been for about four years. I would say, however, that if a name does not occur in the casualty lists, that person can be assumed to be relatively OK.

**What about Tom Roper?**

Yes, 'OK' is probably not the right term there, is it? Well, 'not a casualty'.

**'Yet'.**

'At this stage', yes.

**Are you trying to keep people out of the central city area?**

Yes, we are at the moment, obviously.

**How are you doing this?**

We have a public transport system which has achieved this miracle for quite some time.

**How does that work?**

You buy your bus ticket in a chemist or a newsagency.

**You buy your ticket in a chemist or newsagency?**

Yes.

**Where do you buy your newspapers?**

In a swimming pool.

**Where do you swim?**

In a library.

**Things haven't been going all that well recently, have they?**

Well, things could, frankly, have gone a little better lately, yes.

**Where do you think it all went wrong?**

In retrospect it probably wasn't a great idea to try to run a merchant bank.

**Using public money?**

Yes. There may well be some mistakes we haven't made. I just can't recall too many of them as I speak to you now.

**What did you lose?**

On the merchant bank?

**Yes.**

About one-and-a-half billion dollars.

**Didn't you also try to run an insurance company with public money?**

That was Workcare. Mind you, Workcare is a brilliant idea, bold concept.

**But what did that lose?**

About three billion.

**Mr Cain, would you like to say goodbye to anyone?**

*(sound of explosion)*

God that's close. They're getting our range. Can we finish soon?

**Yes. Would you like to say a quick goodbye to the electorate?**

No. Let's not get hysterical. Let's give it a day or so.

# A New Leader

**Dr John Hewson, Leader
of the Federal Opposition**

**Dr Hewson, first of all, congratulations.**

Thank you very much.

**How are you settling in?**

It's a bit early to say. I've only just got here.

**No, I meant as Leader of the Party?**

Oh, I see. Things are going pretty well, I think. We've got a new team, of course, a new team, a good team, a bold team and a very strong team.

**Did you get the team that you wanted?**

Actually, we haven't got the full team yet.

**When will you get it?**

Very soon, I hope. I do expect it will be a very good team indeed.

**How much of the team have you got so far?**

At the moment we've just got two members of the team.

**And who are they?**

Myself, obviously, and Mr ... Mr ...

**Reith?**

Yes. Barry Reith.

**Peter.**

Peter Barry.

**Peter Reith.**

Yes. There are several of us at the moment. It's just a question of filling it out a little.

**Were you disappointed that you didn't get Australia's next Prime Minister as your deputy?**

Let me say I think Andrew Peacock still has a very major contribution to make to the Liberal Party.

**How will he be best used, do you think?**

Difficult to say at the moment. Possibly in a display case, I think, somewhere in the foyer.

**Has he asked for a specific position?**

He has asked if he can work the lift.

**Can he?**

No, not on the evidence available so far.

**What about Mr Howard?**

Well, the lift will obviously need to go up as well as down.

**Mr Chaney?**

Pretty rigorous safety requirements in lifts these days, you know.

**Have you thought about putting Andrew in the Victorian State Parliament?**

Why would we do that?

**He keeps winning elections in Victoria.**

Yes, but we've got a leader in Victoria.

**No, you haven't. You've got Alan Brown.**

How bad are things for the Labor Party in Victoria?

**Tom Roper's the Treasurer.**

Good God, is that legal?

**I don't think he's allowed to sign anything.**

Oh, Andrew would give him a really good shake.

**How do you feel about the prospect of working with Ian Sinclair as head of the National Party?**

It would be most inappropriate for me to make any comment about that. That's an internal matter for the National Party. They will obviously meet and make their own deliberations. We'll be more than happy to work with whatever leader is thrown up by due process.

**Will you be meeting with them?**

Yes, we'll meet with them on Monday.

**At what time?**

About feeding time.

**Dr Hewson thanks for joining us.**

Thank you.

*(getting up)* **How was that?**

Pretty good.

**Do you think you'll be able to find your own way out?**

Settle down. I've just found my way in.

# A Tragic Loss

**Mr John Stone, Defeated Senator**

**Mr Stone, you've lost your bid to get into the House of Representatives.**

It is beginning to look that way at the moment, although, of course, the postal votes are not all in yet.

**How many postal votes are outstanding?**

There are one hundred and twenty-eight postal votes currently outstanding in the electorate at the moment.

**How many of those do you need?**

About fourteen thousand.

**It's going to be touch and go.**

It's a cliff-hanger, no doubt about it. We expected a close election, a very close election indeed.

**Is it as close as you expected?**

It's a little bit closer than we expected, actually.

**By how much?**

By about fourteen thousand.

**So you've decided to go back to your old job in the Senate?**

Yes, I'm always on the lookout for ways of serving the Australian people.

**I have heard it said (not by me, incidentally—I have great respect for you) that you promised you wouldn't do that, that you felt that it contravened the spirit of the Australian electoral system.**

You've heard criticism?

**I have.**

Implied criticism or direct personal criticism?

**Implied.**

Really? That surprises me. I'm anxious to get back in because I have a great deal of unfinished business to do in the Parliament.

**Like what?**

Like the ID card.

**But I thought you were against the ID card?**

I was opposed to the Labor Party's ID card. The ID card I'm proposing is a voluntary ID card.

**How does it work?**

Well, privileges accrue to certain card-holders.

**Like what?**

Well, it would work at the races. For instance, if you backed a horse at the TAB and it didn't win, you could take your card down to the TAB and get your money back.

**What's it called?**

It's called the John Stone Card.

**So you actually get two go's at everything?**

You get a minimum of two go's at everything, possibly three or four; it depends on how many horses you backed.

**Would it work, say, at the pictures?**

Yes. You'd just come out and say you didn't enjoy the picture very much, show them the card and get your money back.

**So, you just need the ticket.**

Yes. You just need to prove beyond any doubt that you are in fact John Stone.

**How many of these would be made?**

We don't know at the moment. The legislation is at a very early draft stage.

**How many?**

Planned?

**Yes.**

At the moment?

**Yes.**

One.

**And who's going to get that?**

No idea. It would be very inappropriate for me to comment on that at this stage.

**Mr Stone, thanks for joining us ...** *(puts papers down)* **What are you going to do over Easter?**

I'll have a pretty quiet time. I'll probably sleep for the first couple of days.

**What will you do then?**

Then I'll get up.

**When?**

On the third day.

**Business as usual?**

Yes. Stick to your principles.

**Stick to your what?**

Sorry, I was just clearing my throat.

# The Consumption Tax Debate

**Dr John Hewson, Leader of the Federal Opposition**

**Dr Hewson, thank you for finding the studio.**

Thank you. It's a great pleasure to arrive, and thank you for inviting me.

**You're working towards some proposal for a consumption tax.**

What I actually said was, we are looking for a scenario where, under certain circumstances, it may not be completely inappropriate to introduce some sort of very broadly based consumption tax at some future time.

**How does a consumption tax work?**

*No, look …* (conspiratorially) *What you do is … I pretend that we're not going to introduce a consumption tax and you try to trick me into denying that we're actually going to do it. That's the way it works.*

**Dr Hewson, could you describe a consumption tax?**

Why don't you do that? I say, ' We're not going to introduce one,' and then … I'll help you, I'll give you a few clues. I'll leak you some John Elliott stuff. Then I'll say, 'Yes, of course, there is some support in some quarters for some sort of tax at some future time.' That's the way the consumption tax argument works. Read it out.

**What is a consumption tax, Dr Hewson? Is it a tax on**

**consumption?**

Yes, of course it is.

**There are three things you can do with money, aren't there? You can save it, spend it or invest it.**

That's right.

**The poor don't save much.**

They don't save a whole lot, no.

**Do they make a lot of investments?**

I don't think they're a very big player in the market currently. No.

**So, a consumption tax is applied to money that is spent.**

Correct.

**Let me put this to you: if a family has an income, after paying income tax, of five hundred dollars a week, and it costs them five hundred dollars a week for rent, food and running the car; they have no investments, no savings; what percentage of their income attracts a consumption tax?**

Roughly?

**Roughly.**

Roughly one hundred percent.

**What are you going to do with all this money?**

We're going to give tax relief.

**To whom?**

To people who save and invest ... Why don't you try to trick me into a denial? That's the way the consumption argument works. Trick me into a denial that we're actually planning to introduce it. That's the way it works.

**You want to play a game?**

Yes. Why don't you play the game properly?

**I don't want to play a game.**

You big sook.

**I beg your pardon?**

You're a big baby.

# Big Things in the Wind

**The Hon. John Button,
Minister for Industry,
Technology and
Commerce**

**Senator Button, how are things going?**
Very well indeed.

**The car industry is going well?**
Going very well, thanks. Yes.

**The protection debate going well?**
Yes. Going very well indeed. Couldn't be better.

**You're pretty happy with the way things are going?**
Yes.

**No thought of getting out then?**
No.

**None?**
Out of what?

**Out of the Government. No thoughts of retiring?**
Of retiring?

**Yes.**

No thoughts of that at all. No.

**There was some suggestion that you might retire.**

I read that, but no—no thoughts of giving it away at this stage.

**What's that on your back?**

In fact, quite the reverse. I'm taking on more work.

**What's that thing on your back?**

It's a bag. I'm going to be taking on so much more work, perhaps a couple more portfolios, that they've given me a bag to put it all in.

**Where did you get it?**

Graham Richardson gave it to me.

**Has anyone else got one?**

Yes, Ralph Willis has got one too.

**Exactly the same?**

Yes.

**He's going to be given a lot of added responsibility too?**

Yes.

**Just you and Ralph Willis?**

Yes.

**How does it work?**

The bag? Well, you wait until Senator Richardson opens the door …

**What do you do when he's got the door open?**

You take a deep breath, jump through the door and you've got ten seconds to name all the portfolios you want.

**You and Ralph?**

Yes.

**What happens after ten seconds?**

You pull this cord.

**Pull the cord?**

Yes, you just pull that.

**You know what it is, don't you?**

Yes, it's a cord.

**It's a parachute.**

What's a parachute?

**It's a big sort of tent that opens up above your head ...**

Yes, I know what a parachute is—what are you saying is a parachute? You're telling me the added-responsibility bag is a parachute?

**Yes. Where's the Cabinet meeting?**

I don't know.

**Tell me where it is.**

I'm not going to tell you where it is.

**Is it in a plane?**

It could be.

**Did they give you anything else?**

Yes. There's a boat you blow up and a whistle to attract attention.

**In the meeting?**

Yes.

**What's the boat for?**

It's not a boat.

**You said it was a boat.**

It's only a boat if you blow it up.

**What is it if you don't blow it up?**

Ralph Willis.

# Gallipoli

**The Hon. Bob Hawke,
Prime Minister of
Australia**

*(This interview took place in flight on the return trip to Australia from
the 75th anniversary of the landing at Anzac Cove on 25 April 1915.)*

**Mr Hawke, it's been quite something this week, hasn't it?**

It's been fantastic. It's been one of the great things you could ever
go through as an Australian. I wouldn't have missed it for the
world.

**What do you think is the significance of the Gallipoli
experience?**

It's a unique experience in Australian history. A lot of lessons. I
think the main lesson is that we as Australians have got to control
our own destiny. We must never again allow ourselves to be put in
the position of being ordered to do things by other people—not our
idea, we don't control it, and frequently we're not even told the full
story. It's a unique experience and that's a very valuable lesson.

**Is the experience unique, though?**

Totally unique in Australian history.

**What about Bullecourt?**

Aside from Bullecourt. Bullecourt was very like it.

**Fromelles?**

And Fromelles, yes. Aside from Bullecourt and Fromelles, totally unique.

**And what about the Somme?**

And the Somme. Take those three out and it's unique.

**Passchendale?**

Well, take the First War out, then. It's completely unique aside from the First War.

**But what about Singapore?**

And Singapore. First War and Singapore—take them out and it's a totally unique experience.

**Cassino?**

And Cassino. Well, take the Second War out as well, take both Wars out. Outside war, it is a totally unique experience.

**What about Maralinga?**

Outside war and Maralinga, obviously, but the lesson's the same at all times. We as Australians have got to control our own destiny. We must never again get in the position of being ordered to do things by a lot of other people.

**On another subject, why is the consumption tax debate back on the agenda?**

The OECD wants us to introduce one.

**Why don't we export more wheat?**

The Americans won't allow it.

**Why don't we sell more beef?**

The Japanese don't want us to.

**What's happening at Nurrunga?**

I don't know, I haven't seen the forecast.

**North-West Cape?**

Nobody knows what's happening there.

**Finally, Mr Hawke, what about the boys who never came back, the Diggers who never returned? What do you think they would think of Australia's position now?**

I don't know, it's difficult to say. I'd be speculating.

**Well speculate. Would they be for it or against it?**

Dead against it, I would think.

**Yes.** *(looks out porthole)* **What's that big thing out there?**

That? That's a wing. There's another one out the other side.

**Where?**

*(both look)*

Well, there was earlier.

# A Valuable Contribution

**The Hon. Peter Walsh,
Former Federal Finance
Minister**

**Mr Walsh, you've left the Hawke Ministry.**

Yes. I have.

**What are you doing now?**

Well, I'm still in the Parliament, of course.

**Doing what?**

Just trying to be of whatever assistance I can.

**In what respect?**

Trying to be of whatever help seems practicable. I have a fair bit more time now that I'm not on the front bench. I've always been a fairly active person. I just like to lend a hand if I feel I can be of some use.

**You like to help others.**

I think we all do.

**It's a personal need, I suppose.**

Yes. I think it is. You're absolutely right. We all like to feel we are being useful.

**How have you been helping?**

Well, I've been trying to get the spineless little ape who runs things at the moment to make a few decisions and get his hands up where we can see them.

### Have you been helping Mr Keating?

Yes, I have—slippery little mongrel, but I'm doing what I can. At least he's got a brain. He'd be a lot better Prime Minister than the jelly-backed little wimp they've got at the moment. Although, he is going to have to make some very difficult decisions about spending cuts or some thug like Richardson's going to grab the wheel and we'll be in the ditch quick-smart.

### You don't like Senator Richardson, I take it.

He's not a bad sort of a bloke, as right-wing opportunists completely devoid of any sort of principle go. It's just that I'm not quite sure at the moment that what this country needs is a government run by a lot of vote-crazed, semi-green wallopers from the New South Wales Right.

### What about Big Business?

We've all had a fair sort of look at the Festival of St Onan in recent years, and I think if Personality-Defect Hawke can get his mind off trying to get the ethnic mafia to propose marriage to him and put some time into the morality of the people he's in bed with already, the world will be a better place, frankly.

### But you like to keep away from personal criticism, don't you?

Yes, wherever possible.

### Mr Walsh, thanks for joining us.

I beg your pardon.

### Senator Walsh, thanks for joining us.

Thank you.

# Charades

**The Hon. John Button, Minister for Industry, Technology and Commerce**

**Senator Button, how do you think things are going?**

Look, let me make it clear—I'm prepared to answer questions that relate directly to the portfolio of Industry, but I'm not going to be drawn into any general speculative comment. I tried that last time and we haven't been able to use the fan for nearly a fortnight.

**Is the Car Plan going to be affected by the Ford recall?**

No. As I understand it they are only recalling a very small number of vehicles.

**How small?**

About seventy thousand.

**A small number of seventy thousand?**

Very small number of about seventy thousand vehicles, for some very minor modifications, as I understand it.

**What was the fault?**

It wasn't a fault. 'Fault' is the wrong word—please stop using it. It is not a fault, it's a very minor modification in certain models.

**What is it?**

Something to do with the steering. It's a technical thing.

**Where is the steering wheel?**

It's in the boot, but only in certain models.

**What about the imported ones?**

The imported models are fine. Go ahead.

**On another subject, were you consulted about the twenty percent foreign ownership ceiling for TV?**

No. I wasn't, but I've got very great faith in the Minister, Kerry Beazley. Kerry's done his homework very well and, frankly, I think he's made the right decision. We need to decide in this country whether we want our television to be dominated by foreigners.

**What was the alternative?**

Well, you can read a newspaper dominated by foreigners.

**Radio?**

Yes. Listen to that—dominated by foreigners.

**Minister, can I ask you your opinion of the recent performance of the Treasurer, Mr Keating?**

No. You can't. I'm not going to speak about that at all. I've made that perfectly plain. How clear do you want it to be? I'm not going to say anything.

**Senator Button, with respect, you must have a view.**

I'm not going to tell you my view. I'm going to keep my view to …

**Senator Button, you are the third highest minister in the country. You can't very well pretend not to have a view about the current macroeconomic climate.**

I'm not going to say anything.

**Can you give us some indication of it?**

*(Senator Button holds up three fingers)*

**Three words.**

*(Senator Button holds up two fingers)*

**Second word ...**

*(Senator Button flaps his elbows)*

**Er ... hen ...**

*(indicates rooster's comb)*

**male hen ... rooster.**

*(points up)*

**Rooster ... rooster ... up ... up rooster ... rooster-up.**

*(holds up one finger)*

**First word ...**

*(makes circle with hands)*

**Whole ... entire ... complete.**

*(indicates correct)*

**Complete rooster-up.**

Complete rooster-up! Good grief—I'll give you another go. *(hands indicate movement of clock)*

**Er ... er ... clock.**

*(pulls ear)*

**Sounds like clock. Cock! Complete rooster cock.**

Complete rooster cock! *(gives up in disgust, looks away)* Next!

# The Governor

### The Hon. Paul Keating, Treasurer of Australia

**Mr Keating, you enjoy running things. You like being the top dog, don't you?**

Well, it's not bad. It's a very big job—I'm not going to run away from that—but I like to think I've had a pretty good first week.

**You've got a lot of responsibility.**

Yes, but there's no use running away from it. That's the job.

**How many prisoners do you have overall?**

We've got about sixty prisoners in the main block and another two hundred out in the rehabilitation farm area.

**Is John Button there?**

Yes. All the Senators are there. John Button's actually a model prisoner. We did catch him trying to smuggle a radio in at one point, but he's a very good boy now.

**They're not allowed to listen to news from outside?**

Yes, they are. They're just not allowed to broadcast news to the outside.

**Is Senator Tate down there as well?**

He is now, yes. We had a bit of a problem with Senator Tate—he went over the wall in broad daylight—but we've got him again now.

**Where was he?**

He was down in the main street saying he was Michael Tate, that he'd gone over the wall in broad daylight, and did anyone want to have their photograph taken with him.

**Where is he now?**

We've bricked him into the ablutions area now.

**And is Senator Walsh down there as well?**

Yes. We did have a slight problem with Senator Walsh—he was caught trying to pass notes to one of the other prisoners.

**What about?**

He was trying to tunnel his way out of his cell and he had a few problems.

**Where did he hide the dirt?**

Well, that was the problem he mentioned in his note.

**What happened? Did he get out?**

He got out of his own cell and tunnelled his way very successfully for some distance, but rather tragically for Senator Walsh, he came up in solitary.

**And did you find him?**

Well, we found him in solitary, but he heard us coming and tunnelled his way back down to his cell.

**Did you cover the hole in the end?**

Yes. We covered the hole in both ends. You haven't heard a lot from him in the last week, have you?

**No, that's true. Where's John Button at the moment?**

We put him in the sewing-of-mailbags area—he's taken over the whole division and apparently he's reforming their work practices.

**Successfully?**

Very successfully. Apparently it's going very well.

**And how many mailbags are they turning out now?**

I don't know. We buy our mailbags from South Korea.

**Why?**

It's cheaper.

**How do you feed the prisoners?**

We slide the food in under the door in most cases, although we've got to make an exception with Senator Ray, of course, and with Senator Richardson.

**What happens with them?**

We slide the door in under the food.

**Finally, Mr Keating, where do you keep Mr Hawke?**

Mr Hawke's in hospital at the moment.

**Is that impregnable?**

Well, that's what they're trying to fix.

# Concerning His Prostate Operation

**The Hon. Bob Hawke,
Prime Minister of
Australia**

**Prime Minister, you look great. How do you feel?**

I'm a danger to shipping.

**The doctors are pleased with your progress?**

The doctors are absolutely delighted with my progress. All the indications are favourable. Yes.

**With respect, that's the second time you've recovered this year, isn't it?**

That's extremely amusing.

**What actually happened, Mr Hawke?**

You mean the operation?

**Yes.**

Oh, I don't want to talk about the operation. Let's talk about politics. You don't want to hear about an operation.

**Why not?**

Well, basically, it's plumbing. That's all it is. It's a very standard piece of carpentry and plumbing. Let's not bother with that. Let's talk about something else.

**I just want to know precisely what happened during the operation.**

I'd rather not talk about it. Can't we discuss something else?

**Prime Minister, it's all very well going to press conferences and joking about small member's bills and the like. I think the public's got a right to know.**

I did make some flippant remarks of a very childish nature prior to … I suppose I was a bit jumpy before the operation. I deeply regret those remarks now, of course.

**Were you embarrassed?**

I suppose I was a little bit embarrassed, yes. It's just not something I knew how to do and I suppose I made a little bit of a fool of myself, but I don't want to go through analysis. If you really want to know what happened in the operation, I can tell you.

**I'd like that. Go ahead, please.**

In lay terms—without getting too technical about it—first of all, they knock you out, obviously. The next thing they do is make a very small incision somewhere in behind the Walshes; they pin the Tates back; they put the Dawkins out of the way, of course; they run any surplus Jones off into a bucket; and then they get a very small probe and they pull out, in my case, a little tiny Button about the size of the head of a pin.

**What about the performance of Paul Keating?**

Oh, they never get around that far. That doesn't come into it.

**Why not?**

Well, you're lying on your back. How would they do that?

**Oh, I see.**

I haven't explained myself very well. I mean, physiologically they couldn't possibly do that.

**I see.**

You're on your back. They can only get to the top part.

**I see. Right.**

Have you got a pencil?

**Yes.**

Here. I'll show you. *(makes an illustration)* First of all, there's your Dawkins. You've got the Walshes down here.

**Yes.**

They run a little probe up into here.

**Yes.**

They pin these Tate valves back.

**Yes.**

And they pull that out.

**Yes.**

Now, the Keating would be around here.

**Oh, I see.**

How would they get to that?

# Good Numbers

**The Hon. John Dawkins,
Acting Treasurer**

**Mr Dawkins, you were very pleased with the figures this week, weren't you?**

We were very pleased with these figures. These are very good numbers indeed.

**There was some suggestion that you weren't going to get these numbers, wasn't there?**

There was some speculation prior to the numbers coming out, but I've seen a lot of numbers, believe you me—I'm steeped in numbers—and these figures are excellent. These are some of the best numbers I've ever seen. Under the circumstances these numbers are excellent.

**Under what circumstances?**

Under the circumstances of expecting slightly worse numbers than we got.

**How often do the numbers come out?**

They come out quarterly.

**Yes, but how often?**

Oh, about once every three months.

**And how do they work them out?**

A very complicated method. It's all done under strict security up at the Bureau in Canberra.

**What is it?**

It's far too complex to go into in any detail here.

**Mr Dawkins, with respect, if people are going to be paying South American interest rates, I'm sure they can cope with trying to understand why.**

Well, all the numbers are sitting on little stands, and then someone pulls the trigger, and they roll down a huge chute and into a big round barrel.

**Can you see through it?**

Yes. You'd be surprised how few people do, but you can.

**But you can see all the numbers rolling about?**

Oh yes, plenty of colour and movement. And then a big scoop comes down and rolls six of them down six separate chutes, and they end up sitting on little plastic stands.

125

**And then you read them out?**

Well I don't, but a little bloke with a dinner suit and a stipend does.

**And this is how you work out the current account deficit?**

I believe that's what it's called by financial journalists, yes.

**Why do they do that?**

Well, they're financial journalists. That's why they see things.

**But they do graphs and flow charts and debt-to-GDP analysis based on these figures.**

Well, they can't very well say it's just a chook raffle and we spit the numbers out, can they?

**They could do that.**

They could, but they don't.

**Some do that.**

Yes, but we've got their names, and they were against deregulation when it was brought in.

**Aren't you now regulating certain industries again?**

We are in one or two cases, yes.

**Like what?**

Well, for instance, the stable-door industry requires some attention, but we're not in a hurry to do that.

**Why not?**

We've got to get the horse-bolting legislation through the Senate first.

**Mr Dawkins, we've run out of time. Thanks for joining us.**

Good evening.

**126** **I was just going to ask you ...** *(looks surprised)*

Hello? *(Mr Dawkins voice is muffled—he is sporting a huge hat which has slipped down and is now obscuring his entire head and face)*

**Mr Dawkins, I was just going to ask you about your hat.**

Hello? *(barely audible)*

**Mr Dawkins why do you wear a hat?**

Hello. I can't see your lips moving. Where are you? Hello?

**I'm over here, Mr Dawkins.**

This is a very bad line.

**Why are you wearing a hat these days?**

Have you got a key for this somewhere? Go through my pockets, son, will you—I'm locked in. Do they do breakfast here?

# Wisden

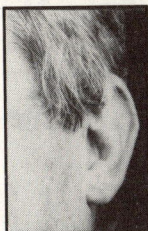

**Mr John Thickness,
English Cricket Writer**

*(This interview took place via satellite from London.)*

**Mr Thickness, you are a contributor to 'Wisden'?**

Yes I am.

**Who wrote the summary of the Ashes series which appears in this year's edition?**

I did.

**Who won the Ashes series?**

I just forget who won it now.

**It wasn't England, was it?**

I don't think it was England, now you come to mention it.

**I think England came second, didn't they?**

They were certainly placed, yes. They put up a very creditable performance.

**They were beaten 4-nil, weren't they?**

I just don't recall the details.

**By Australia.**

I'm sorry?

**What's your real name, Mr Thickness?**

That is my real name.

**Thickness?**

MR Thickness.

**Why do you say that Terry Alderman got a lot of wickets only because he was helped by the umpires?**

Thickness.

**Yes. Why do you say that Terry Alderman got a lot of wickets because he was helped by the umpires?**

Well, all summer he bowled at the batsmen, in test after test, got it past the bat, struck the pad and appealed.

**What's the matter with that?**

In our view the umpires favoured him in the giving of lbw decisions.

**Why did they do that?**

They couldn't see the ball.

**Why not?**

It was travelling too fast.

**Who told you that?**

The batsmen. They were a lot closer than the umpires and apparently they couldn't see it at all.

**Where were the batsmen standing?**

When the ball hit them?

**Yes.**

Right in front of the wickets.

**So they had a pretty good view of proceedings.**

Yes, a far better view than the umpire.

**What part of them was obscuring the wickets at the time?**

Oh, an arm, perhaps part of a shoulder—an ear in one or two cases.

**Do you realise that the Australian trade figures came out today and were slightly down on expectations?**

I didn't know that, no.

**Things were going pretty well until 'Wisden' came out.**

Are you suggesting that your trading performance is in some way indexed to your national sporting ego?

**Isn't yours?**

No.

**Well, why did you write that about Terry Alderman?**

Thickness.

**How's the weather?**

Beautiful.

**That looks like sleet.**

There's just a bit of light sleet falling.

**At what angle?**

It's coming in at about forty-five degrees.

**Will you get any play today?**

Against the Indians?

**Yes.**

Yes, they'll play.

**Why?**

Graham Gooch is on 194.

**Not out?**

Yes. Alderman's not playing.

**I give up.**

*(sings)* There'll always be an England. Will you please stand for the anthem? *(sings)* Land of hope and glory, mother of the free.

# The Cambodian Refugee Question

**The Hon. Bob Hawke,
Prime Minister of
Australia**

**Mr Hawke, I wonder if we could talk about the Immigration Debate that has grown up around the Chinese students you made a special-case argument for when ...**

Hang on ... *(picks up phone)* Barry, rather a long question, son. You might have to go and shift the car ... *(hangs up)* Sorry. Go on.

131

**... when you spoke about your wish that the Immigration Policy could be sufficiently flexible to accommodate some provision for offering sanctuary much greater in the case of ...**

Is this question coming out as a novel?

**Pardon?**

I'd be most interested to read it.

**Can I please finish?**

I'd be delighted if you would, please, yes.

**Where was I?**

You were saying, 'sanctuary much'.

**Sanctuary much for what?**

I don't know, sanctuary much for something.

**Probably for coming along.**

Always a pleasure. Sanct YOU very much.

**Why is there a separate policy for the Chinese students?**

Because they're political refugees.

**As distinct from the Cambodians?**

Yes, who are of course economic refugees.

**Are there a lot of economic refugees?**

In a country where a quarter of the population has been killed by the government?

**Yes.**

Yes, there do tend to be rather a lot of economic refugees under those circumstances.

**People seem very confused by your policy.**

No they're not.

**I'm sorry, they are.**

No they're not. I sorted that out this week. I made a full statement about it.

**You said it was balderdash.**

I said it was BLOODY balderdash.

**What's the difference?**

'Bloody' is more manly—much more manly, 'bloody'. I put 'bloody' in.

**The Chinese students themselves didn't understand your policy.**

Of course they didn't. They're here to study English. You wouldn't expect them to understand it.

**Does it address the distinction between the Chinese stu-**

dents and any other refugees so distressed they're prepared to risk their lives in order to get out of their own countries?

Yes, of course it does.

**And the idea that the Chinese students can stay here, and the ten-year sunset clause?**

Yes. It's all in the policy.

**What does the policy say?**
*(at this point the Prime Minister appears to talk backwards)*

Asdfg mngkflfd qeruiop dfjlrewer sfyhuwopr gpoiurkh ssdfghjkl.

**That doesn't make sense.**

Asdfg mngkflfd qeruiop dfjlrewer sfyhuwopr gpoiurkh ssdfghjkl.

**Mr Hawke, thank you.**

Thank you. I hope you're clear on that now.

**Asdfg mngkflfd qeruiop dfjlrewer sfyhuwopr gpoiurkh ssdfghjkl.**

Yes, by about six goals, I would think. Should be a good game.

# The Annual Premiers' Conference

 **The Hon. Paul Keating,
Treasurer of Australia**

**Mr Keating, did the Premiers' Conference go well?**

Very well. It's a terribly difficult business at the moment, because the policies of the States are sometimes at odds with a continued improvement in the national position. We had a few problems yesterday, but we sorted things out today.

**How did you resolve those issues? Yesterday there was no agreement at all.**

We locked ourselves away. I think everyone realised we had to find an arrangement acceptable to all parties. They're very intelligent people.

**But everyone knew what was going to happen. It's the same every year.**

No it's not. This was a particularly difficult year.

**There's a pattern.**

No there's not.

**Look, you put your foot in yesterday morning.**

Well, that's a pretty crude expression—that's not how it's done. I don't know where you got that.

**Well, you put your foot in.**

I put my foot in?

**Yes.**

What's this about my feet? Where did you get this from?

**Apparently you did it twice, and then you put your other foot in in the afternoon.**

Yes, but I took the first foot out first.

**Which foot was your first foot?**

My left, from memory, but I took it out before I put the other one in.

**What did you do with your right foot?**

I didn't do anything with my right foot.

**Mr Bannon says you shook it.**

Mr Bannon?

**Yes.**

He says I shook my foot?

**Yes. He says you all did.**

Did he shake his?

**Yes. He says he shook it last year, too.**

Shook it where?

**Everywhere. All over the place.**

He shook his foot all over the place?

**Yes, that's what you do, isn't it?**

Are you serious?

**Yes.**

This is the pattern you recognise?

**Yes. You put you left foot in, you put your left foot out, you put your left foot in and you shake it all about. This is the hokey-pokey, isn't it, Mr Keating? You're doing the hokey-pokey?**

We're doing the hokey-pokey?

**It's the same every year. I bet I can tell you what'll happen at next year's Premiers' Conference.**

Don't be ridiculous.

**The States will have to accept revenue cuts in the 1992 fiscal year because of factors bearing on the current account and the need to keep inflation and interest rates in place.**

That's wrong.

**You tell me what's going to happen then.**

We don't know yet.

**Why not?**

We haven't booked the band.

**You must have some idea?**

We've got a few ideas, yes.

**What sort of thing?**

We're going to jump down turn around pick a bale of cotton.

# On the Possibility that Monetarism is the Disease for Which it Claims to be the Cure

**The Hon. Bob Hawke,
Prime Minister of
Australia**

**Mr Hawke, thanks for coming in. Congratulations, incidentally.**

Thanks. What have I done, as a matter of interest?

**On being Malcolm Fraser for a longer period than he was.**

I wouldn't have put it like that, but thanks anyway.

**How would you have put it?**

Malcolm was being Bob Hawke, but for a period considerably less magnificent than my own.

**Do you think Bob Hawke could ever become Robert Menzies?**

Well, I don't know about that. You've got to remember Menzies was Bob Hawke for donkey's years.

**You don't think anyone these days could be Bob Hawke for as long as Menzies was?**

It's difficult to imagine in Australia, but of course overseas you've got people like Lee Kwan Yew, Jomo Kenyatta ...

**How long have they been Bob Hawke?**

About twenty years.

**Margaret Thatcher's been Bob Hawke for three terms in Britain.**

Haile Selassie was Bob Hawke for a long time.

**Wasn't Bob Hawke Haile Selassie for a while there too?**

I was a little bit Selassie as a young man, but only very occasionally.

**You're hardly Selassie at all now.**

I don't have the time.

**Have I spoken to you since the balance of payments figure was announced?**

I don't think so, no.

**It was pretty bad, wasn't it?**

Well, it wasn't good. It could have been better.

**How many bad ones have we had in a row now?**

We've had a few that could have been better.

**How many?**

The last eighty-three of them could have shown some improvement.

**Is there some possibility that monetary policy is actually causing the problems it's supposed to solve?**

Well, that's not very logical, is it?

**Well, monetary policy uses high interest rates to deter people from borrowing.**

Of course it does.

**But when interest rates are high, aren't foreign lenders going to come in?**

I would certainly hope so.

**Doesn't that push up the value of the Australian dollar?**

It could do, yes—in theory.

**Is the Australian dollar high at the moment?**

Yes, it is. There's a flaw in this argument somewhere.

**If the value of the dollar is up, isn't that precisely the best time to import?**

Because you get more for your dollar?

**Yes.**

Yes. Just go back over this from the beginning, will you?

**So isn't the demand for imports going to go up rather than down?**

Yes. I'll spot the deliberate mistake in a minute. Just start the interview again, will you?

**Mr Hawke, congratulations.**

Thank you.

**Isn't monetarism causing the problems it is supposed to fix?**

No—you've lost me. Just go back again, will you?

**Mr Hawke, congratulations.**

Thank you.

**Isn't monetarism causing the problems it is supposed to fix?**

Sorry—just give it to me again, will you?

**Mr Hawke, congratulations.**

Thank you.

**Isn't monetarism causing the problems it is supposed to fix?**

What did you say before that?

**Mr Hawke, congratulations.**

Thank you very much.

# Jockeying for Position

**Mr Peter Reith, Shadow Treasurer of Australia**

**Mr Reith, you've reacted strongly to the trade figures announced today.**

Yes, I have. They're woeful.

**Are they?**

They're terrible. We're in terrible, terrible trouble.

**Are we?**

Oh, dreadful. Awful, dreadful, appalling, awful, dreadful trouble. I am appalled. The position is dreadful.

**Is it horrendous?**

It is, yes. I was horrended earlier today.

**What exactly is wrong at the moment?**

What the figures show is that we've now got ourselves caught between an improved import position and a greatly unimproved export position.

**Both caused by the same mechanism?**

Precisely.

**It sounds awful.**

It is. It's frightful.

**What is the solution? Do we lower interest rates?**

No, we can't afford to take the pressure off demand.

**Do we increase them?**

No, we'll drown in foreign capital if we do that.

**So you agree with Mr Keating?**

No, I oppose Mr Keating.

**Yes, but you agree with what he's doing.**

On interest rates?

**Yes.**

He's got no choice.

**So what should he do?**

They've got to get their act together on Privatisation.

**142** **Well, they were talking about the telecommunications industry this week.**

Yes, but this Megacom's not the way to go.

**Mr Beazley's idea?**

Yes. That's hopeless.

**So you agree with Mr Hawke?**

In backing Mr Keating?

**Yes.**

No. I'm opposed to both of them.

**But you agree with their opposition to Mr Beazley.**

Oh yes.

**It's a good thing Mr Beazley's not running the Government.**

It is indeed.

**Would you look at a consumption tax?**

Yes, we would.

**So you're more in the Senator Button camp?**

No. We think Senator Button should be sacked. He's one of the worst ministers probably anywhere in the world.

**But you agree with him about a consumption tax.**

Yes, of course we do.

**If Senator Button were removed from his portfolio, given that you agree with him on the consumption tax, what portfolio would you give him?**

Oh … *(thinks)* … Industry.

**When will you be releasing your own proposals for economic reform?**

Very soon. We're preparing them at the moment.

**When will you release them?**

As soon as they're ready.

**When will that be?**

Don't know.

**This year?**

Don't know.

**Early next year?**

Don't know.

**Late next year?**

Don't know.

**Middle of next year?**

Don't know.

*(taking some dice from his pocket)* **See if you can throw a six.** Why?

**To start.**

*(taking the dice)* OK. Let's have a go.

*(some time later)* **Sorry, I've got to go. You're welcome to keep trying if you like.**

# The Hidden Agenda

**The Hon. Paul Keating,
Treasurer of Australia**

**Mr Keating, you've announced a major policy shift. Can I ask why this happened?**

No. We haven't announced a policy shift.

**You've abandoned monetary policy.**

We haven't abandoned the policy. We've eased the central mechanism, by all means, but the policy is still there. It's only having the policy that has got us into a position where we can do this.

**So things are going pretty well?**

In the economy?

**Yes.**

Yes, humming like a top.

**What's in the bag?**

Just some fresh underwear.

**It's going pretty well, then?**

You can't be too careful.

**Mr Keating, the policy has just been window-dressing, hasn't it?**

*(holds up sign)* ASK ME ABOUT PRIVATISATION

**The private sector has had negative investment for the last three quarters.**

*(another sign)* PRIVATISATION IS REALLY INTERESTING

**The high interest rates have brought currency speculators into the market and put the dollar up to a point where we can't export anything.**

*(sign)* <u>PLEASE</u> ASK ME ABOUT PRIVATISATION

**And isn't a new Middle East war going to put oil prices up by twenty-five percent?**

*(begs)* Just mention Privatisation. I'll get stuck into the Left for you.

**How are we going to survive a hike in oil prices? Industry has stopped producing and gone into debt management.**

Privatisation!

**And the investment community is hiding under the bed.**

Which brings us to Privatisation, of course. Now what we need to do is reduce public indebtedness to a point where …

**It doesn't bring us to Privatisation at all, Mr Keating.**

Yes it does.

**No, it does not, and I'm not going to be side-tracked.**

*(conspiratorially)* I'll tell you a good story about Graham Richardson.

**There aren't any good stories about Graham Richardson.**

Yes there are.

**No there aren't.**

I've got photos. They're both in shot.

**Look, it doesn't matter who owns Qantas. If they need seven hundred million dollars to buy planes, the money**

**goes to Seattle, Washington.**

*(holds up sign)* YOUR FLY IS UNDONE

**It doesn't matter whether it's private debt or public debt—
that's completely immaterial. It's still Australian debt.**

*(sign)* GOOD EVENING

**Mr Keating, thank you.**

# The Killer

**Mr Alan Brown, Leader of
the Victorian Opposition**

**Mr Brown, thanks for joining us.**

Thank you very much for inviting me to come along and sit with
you in the studio and talk to you under these conditions. I am very
grateful and thank you very much indeed.

**Have you ever been on television before?**

Oh, yes. Yes indeed. I've been interviewed on the steps of Parliament
a number of times. I just forget the dates.

**When are you going to take over government in Victoria?**

I don't know.

**You don't know?**

I've got no idea.

**You're pretty well positioned at the moment to do it, aren't
you?**

Yes, I'm very comfortable now and thank you very much indeed for
inviting me in.

**I mean, the Labor Party does seem to have a lot of prob-
lems—that's what I'm saying.**

Well, obviously you'd have to ask the Labor Party about that, but from my position I think they're going through a bit of a rough patch. I don't think there's any doubt about that.

**Isn't this something you can capitalise on? Isn't this exactly the time for Alan Brown to come surging out of nowhere like a wolf on the fold?**

While the Labor Party are experiencing all these difficulties?

**Yes. The Premier has resigned, the public image of the Labor Party is dreadful, the Treasury is taking in wash-ing—'Alan Brown, come on down'.**

Yes. You think so?

**Mr Brown, I'm trying to help you. Do you understand what I'm doing? Don't fight it, just agree with me.**

Yes.

**I mean, they're unstable. You could get in there and offer sensible management and responsible leadership.**

How would we do that?

**Well, haven't you got a political model, a hero you could imitate?**

Oh, I see—someone I admire whom I could copy.

**Yes.**

Yes. That's a good idea. I'll do that. That's a good idea. Thanks.

**Who is it?**

Yes. I'll do that now. That's a good idea. Thanks. Good.

**Who is it? Whose lead are you prepared to follow?**

Barrie Unsworth.

**Mr Brown, thanks.**

Thank you very much. It's been really nice. I've enjoyed myself a lot.

**You haven't done this a lot, have you?**

I've done it on the steps of Parliament a fair bit, but I've never done it sitting down, 'in situ', in the sitting …

**… position.**

… position.

—